BUSINESS
READING
SKILLS

Joe Cooper

BUSINESS READING SKILLS

MICHAEL CARRIER

Nelson

Thomas Nelson and Sons Ltd
Nelson House   Mayfield Road
Walton-on-Thames   Surrey
KT12 5PL   UK

51 York Place
Edinburgh
EH1 3JD   UK

Thomas Nelson (Hong Kong) Ltd
Toppan Building 10/F
22A Westlands Road
Quarry Bay   Hong Kong

© Michael Carrier
First published by Thomas Nelson and Sons Ltd 1985
ISBN 0-17-555660-1

NPN 9 8 7 6 5
Printed in Hong Kong

Acknowledgements
The author and publishers are grateful to the many
firms and institutions who have given permission for
copyright material to be reproduced. All sources are
acknowledged in the text. The text for Unit 11 is
reproduced by kind permission of the British
Association for Commercial and Industrial Education
(BACIE), 16 Park Crescent, London W1N 4AP, England.
Cover text extracted from *The Times*, by permission.

CONTENTS

key: ▤ = American English   ⚡ = British English

5

Here are some notes on how you can use this book. *Business Reading Skills* is designed to help you read and understand the business papers, texts and documents you need for your job. It gives you practice in reading quickly, to get an idea of the meaning of a text, and it gives you practice in reading carefully and intensively, to get all the information out of the text.

Here are the types of text you can find in the book:

business letters
business advertisements
business brochures
management training documents
newspaper articles on business
magazine articles on business
company reports

You can study the texts in any order—you do not have to work through the book from Unit 1 to Unit 35. But the texts at the beginning of the book are shorter and easier to read than the texts at the end of the book. There are 35 texts in the book, and each one has a page of notes and exercises. These are described below.

Before you read a text, you should look at the **vocabulary** and **skim** sections. Then, when you have read the text once, try to answer the **comprehension** questions. Look at the **reference** and **language** notes, and read the text again. Now try to answer the **inference** and **reference** questions.

When you think you understand the text, look at the **opinion** and **writing** sections, and do some written work on the text.

EXERCISES

A Before you read the text

1 VOCABULARY

This section gives explanations of difficult words or phrases in the text. They are also listed at the back of the book.

2 SKIM

These are questions to answer after you have read the text quickly. Look at these questions before you read the text, so you know what you have to find out.

B After you have read the text

3 COMPREHENSION

These are questions on the information in the text. They test how well you have understood the text.

4 INFERENCE

These are questions on the hidden meanings of the text. They ask you to look for information or opinions which are not written in the text, but which can be understood 'behind' the writer's words.

5 REFERENCE

These notes help you to find out about names, places and other references in the text which might make the meaning unclear.

6 LANGUAGE

These notes explain a language point from the text, and ask you to practise it.

7 OPINION

These questions suggest topics to discuss with other students, and ideas about the text that you might agree with or disagree with. If you are working on your own, you can practise writing your opinions down.

8 WRITING

These are writing exercises about the information or opinions contained in the text. They help you to practise writing reports, letters, requests, etc in English.

ANSWERS

The answers to the reference and inference questions are printed in the answer key at the back of the book

GLOSSARY

There is a glossary at the back of the book. It contains all the words that are explained in the vocabulary notes, and tells you which unit you can find the explanation in.

DICTIONARY

It is not always a good idea to use a dictionary when you are reading. Often, you can get the wrong meaning of a word from a dictionary. Try and understand the text without a dictionary at first and always do the skim exercises before looking at a dictionary. It is important to learn how to understand a text without worrying about every word that you do not know. You can often work out what a word means, from the meaning of the other words.

To the teacher

Business Reading Skills is designed to develop and practise the skills of both extensive and intensive reading. The texts are selected to interest and motivate a wide range of business-oriented learners of English. The basic criterion for the choice of the texts is whether or not the learner can imagine him/herself having to read this text, or something very similar, in a business or occupational situation.

The texts come from the following sources:

business letters   newspaper articles
advertisements   magazine articles
business brochures   company reports
management training documents

Both British and American sources are represented in the selection of the texts, and are identified by the symbols ⚡ and 🇺🇸. Most of the texts are quite short, as students should not be overloaded with vocabulary that will not prove useful in their work. Nor should they be demotivated by having to study long, dry and dense texts.

The units are organised into an approximate grading sequence—there is a progression of difficulty from beginning to end of the book. Bearing that in mind, however, the units can be studied in any order.

The notes and exercise types remain relatively constant through the book, so that students develop a familiarity and confidence with the material and know what is expected of them.

EXERCISE TYPES

Each unit contains material under the following section headings:

1 VOCABULARY

Explanations of difficult lexis and phrases, to be studied before reading to avoid hesitation over unknown vocabulary. For ease of reference, all lexis explained in this section is listed alphabetically with unit numbers at the back of the book.

2 SKIM

Students should read these skim questions (often known as 'signpost questions') before reading, in order to give purpose and focus for the first, extensive, reading. It should be emphasised that the first reading is for gist, and students should not stop at every unknown word. The answers to these questions are easily found, without detailed lexical knowledge. This should help to boost student confidence in reading.

3 COMPREHENSION

After the first skim or gist reading of the text, students should read for more detailed comprehension, using the questions in this section both as a signpost to show what information to look for, and as a check on what they have read. The teacher can decide whether to direct the

students to look at these questions *before* or only *after* reading the text again.

4 INFERENCE

The questions here direct students to search for and retrieve information which is not explicitly stated, but rather implied by the information or the attitudes contained in the text. This skill of 'reading between the lines' is especially important in the world of business, where, in many cases, subtle and diplomatic criticisms or refusals are expressed implicitly rather than explicitly.

5 REFERENCE

Most texts contain cultural or factual references which a native speaker will recognise, but which might confuse non-native learners and undermine their confidence in being able to understand such texts. The notes and questions in the reference section either give students the necessary information or direct them to find out or speculate about the names, places, acronyms, and other references that occur. In many cases it is not so much necessary for the students to understand the reference, as to understand that it *is* a reference—a reference that they cannot be expected to understand without background knowledge or further study.

6 LANGUAGE

This section provides lexical or structural practice of language points that are used in the text and which could possibly cause difficulties. The teacher may want to supplement this section to provide extended practice for the students.

7 OPINION

The tasks and questions in this section can be used as a stimulus to discussion and pairwork in the class, or as a complement to the writing tasks which follow. They also serve as a further check on comprehension of the attitudes and information in the text.

8 WRITING

These writing tasks follow from the information and the topic of the text, and direct students to practise writing business reports, memos, letters, promotional copy and so on. It is beyond the scope of this book to *teach* the skills involved.

METHODS

As described in the notes to the exercises, the students are expected to read the texts more than once, in both extensive (skimming, gist-reading) and intensive (detailed) reading phases. In the first phase, the notes to sections 1 and 2 are studied prior to reading and are discussed afterwards. Other problems in the first reading can be dealt with at this stage, but only briefly. It is important that students realise that they are expected only to get the general idea of the meaning of the text in the first reading, and they must not get discouraged if they do not understand everything. It must be pointed out to them that they must not expect to understand every word—they must develop skills of inferring meaning, predicting meaning from context, and simply guessing what a word may mean. They must *not* be encouraged to look up all unknown words in a dictionary.

The second phase involves intensive reading of the text, several times, in sections and as a whole, in order to retrieve the various pieces of detailed information required by the exercises in sections 3 to 8. Tasks 3, 4 and 5 are more directly related to the text and should be completed before going on to tasks 6, 7 and 8, which develop comprehension of the text in other directions. Task 4 is often more difficult than 5, and so can be done after it. Task 8 gives the students the chance to relate the form and content of the text to their own working environment, and therefore it may often be advisable for the teacher to reformulate task 8 to suit each group of students.

The answers to the inference and reference questions are given in the key at the back of the book.

MANUFACTURERS OF LIGHT ENGINEERING TOOLS

SPEIRS and WADLEY LTD

ADDERLEY ROAD, HACKNEY
LONDON E.8
TELEPHONE 01-900 1010

Woldal Incorporated,
Broadway,
New York,
U.S.A.

Date   11th August, 19..

Invoice No.   124

QUANTITY	DESCRIPTION	AMOUNT	
400	Electric Power Drills Model LM 425. 2 speed (900 r.p.m. & 2400 r.p.m.) 425 watt high-torque motor. 2 chucks - 12.5 mm & 8 mm - supplied with each drill.		
	Ex-works price £10.00 each	£4000	00
	All freight charges and export packing ..	96	00
	Insurance from warehouse to warehouse ...	12	00
	C.I.F. New York Total	£4108	00

Marks
& Nos.

Packed in 5 wooden cases - 80 per case.

Import Licence No. LHDL No. 22 19..

SW
WOL.
   INC.
NEW
   YORK

1 TO 5

per pro Speirs and Wadley Ltd.

A Look at these sections before you read the text:

1 VOCABULARY

drill machine to make holes
torque a force which makes something turn
chuck end part of drill
ex-works price at the factory (without transport)
warehouse place to store goods

Now read the text and answer the skim questions

2 SKIM

Find out from the text:
a who is receiving these goods?
b what is the basic cost per item of these goods?

B Look at these sections after reading the text:

3 COMPREHENSION

a What does this company make, as well as drills?
b How will the drills get to America?
c What special features does the drill have?

4 INFERENCE

a An import licence is mentioned. Why is this necessary?
b What are the 'Marks & Nos.' shown in the left-hand column?
c Why is the drill called the LM 425 model?

5 REFERENCE

a Find out what these references mean:
   CIF   per pro   rpm
b What is the difference between Ltd and Inc?
c What does 12.5mm mean?

6 LANGUAGE

There are often several different words which have the same or a similar meaning. Find out the differences between:
a case/crate/carton/box
b parcel/package/packet/pack
Write a sentence for each word to show the different meanings.

7 OPINION

a The freight costs are very low—about 2.4% of the cost of the goods. What do you think is the reason for this?
b Why should an American company want to buy drills from a British company? What advantages could there be?
c What sort of products would you expect from a company that makes light engineering tools? What would heavy engineering tools be?

8 WRITING

a You work for Woldal. Write a telex to confirm that you have received the goods.
b You work for Woldal. Thirty five of the drills have been damaged in transit. Write a letter to Speirs and Wadley to complain about this. Give details of the damage and indicate what action you think Speirs and Wadley should take.
c You work for Speirs and Wadley. Reply to the complaint from Woldal about some drills damaged by the shipping company.

CIVIL ENGINEERING

Incorporating Public Works Review

Morgan-Grampian (Construction Press) Limited · 30 Calderwood Street · Woolwich · London SE18 6QH · Tel: 01-855 7777

Re: CE/B1/2.   November, 19 . .

Dear Sir,

Recently we sent you a copy of the September issue
of CIVIL ENGINEERING, together with the opportunity
of receiving your own personally addressed copy,
entirely free of charge, every month.

The response to date has been extremely good, but
we do not appear to have heard from you, so in case
the original application card has gone astray, I
enclose another one with this letter.   Your
satisfactory completion of this will enable me to
look forward to welcoming you as a regular reader
of CIVIL ENGINEERING.

Yours faithfully,

Graham Beardwell

Graham Beardwell,
PUBLISHER.

Enc.

Registration: London 730189 Registered Office: 30 Calderwood Street London SE18 6QH   Telex: 896238 Telegraphic Address: Industpress · Ldn

A Look at these sections before you read the text:

1 VOCABULARY

civil not military
incorporating including
issue edition
astray lost

2 SKIM

a How much does this magazine cost?
b What is the purpose of the letter?
c What is the job of the person who wrote the letter?

Now read the text and answer the skim questions.

B Look at these sections after reading the text:

3 COMPREHENSION

a What did the magazine publisher send with his last letter?
b What response did the customer give?
c How can the customer get a free supply of the magazine?

4 INFERENCE

a Who was this letter sent to? How was this person chosen?
b Why is this magazine sent free of charge? How are the costs paid for?
c Why does the letter say the response to date has been very good? What effect does the publisher want to have?

5 REFERENCE

a What does Enc. at the bottom of the letter refer to?
b What does the Public Works Review refer to?

6 LANGUAGE

Many of the words in the letter are qualified. Explain in a sentence how the meaning would be different if the qualifying word was not there:
a *personally* addressed copy
b *entirely* free of charge
c *satisfactory* completion
d *regular* reader

7 OPINION

a Do you think a magazine is worthwhile if it is offered free? Would you be interested in it?
b If the customer did not reply to the letter in September, he was probably not interested in the magazine. Why do you think the publisher writes again?
c The letter says, 'The response to date has been extremely good'. Do you think this is true? Why?/Why not?

8 WRITING

a Write a letter to the publisher, explaining why you are (or are not) interested in receiving the magazine.
b Imagine you are the publisher of a magazine which has articles about a particular industry. Write a letter to customers trying to persuade them to take the magazine.

BP discovered a new site for their annual meeting at London's Barbican.

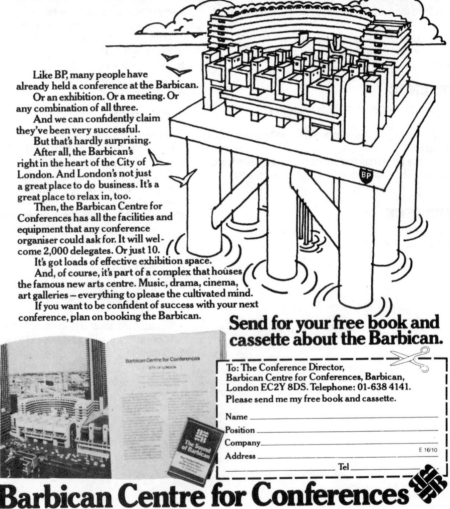

Like BP, many people have already held a conference at the Barbican. Or an exhibition. Or a meeting. Or any combination of all three.

And we can confidently claim they've been very successful.

But that's hardly surprising.

After all, the Barbican's right in the heart of the City of London. And London's not just a great place to do business. It's a great place to relax in, too.

Then, the Barbican Centre for Conferences has all the facilities and equipment that any conference organiser could ask for. It will welcome 2,000 delegates. Or just 10.

It's got loads of effective exhibition space.

And, of course, it's part of a complex that houses the famous new arts centre. Music, drama, cinema, art galleries — everything to please the cultivated mind.

If you want to be confident of success with your next conference, plan on booking the Barbican.

Send for your free book and cassette about the Barbican.

To: The Conference Director,
Barbican Centre for Conferences, Barbican,
London EC2Y 8DS. Telephone: 01-638 4141.
Please send me my free book and cassette.

Name _____
Position _____
Company _____
Address _____   E 16/10
_____ Tel _____

Barbican Centre for Conferences

A Look at these sections before you read the text:

1 VOCABULARY

site a place to put something
(to) claim (to) say it is true
delegates members of a conference
effective useful; successful
loads of a lot of
complex a group of buildings
cultivated sophisticated; artistic; well-educated

Now read the text and answer the skim questions.

2 SKIM

a Find out what the Barbican is—a place, a company or what?
b Find three things that happen in the Barbican.

B Look at these sections after reading the text:

3 COMPREHENSION

a What different activities can be combined in the Barbican?
b What will you get if you write to the Barbican office?
c Why is the Barbican in a good position?

4 INFERENCE

a Why is the name of BP used in the advertisement?
b What does the picture mean or suggest?
c Why should the cinema, the art galleries and so on be useful for a business centre?

5 REFERENCE

Find out the meaning of:
a BP
b EC2 (in the address)
c City (as different from city)

6 LANGUAGE

In informal English we use a lot of verbs with prepositions like this:
   . . . all . . . you could **ask for.**
Find out the prepositions that go at the end of these sentences:
a Jim is someone I can get . . . . . .
b That is a decision I cannot put . . . . . .
c There are two more points we must go . . . . . .
d This new business is ready to take . . . . . .

7 OPINION

a Do you think the advertisement, with the drawing and free cassette, make the Barbican seem a serious place for a business meeting?
b What are the disadvantages of having theatres, cinemas and so on in a conference centre like this?
c What do you think will be on the free cassette? Would you listen to it if you received it?

8 WRITING

a Write a letter to the Barbican asking for further details of the conference service.
b Write a memo to your Board of Directors suggesting that your next annual meeting be held in the Barbican. Explain why you think it would be a good idea.

AMERICANS LIKE TO DO BUSINESS BY PHONE. CALL!

Americans want to hear from you. By telephone. Because that's the way they do business.

A two-way conversation gets questions answered.

Decisions made. Right on the spot.

So nobody waits for hours, overnight, or even a week (the way you may with other means of communication), for all the negotiating it takes to close the deal.

So make it your business to talk it over overseas.

Dial direct when you can (no waiting at all). And to be sure you call when Americans are in their offices, use the schedule at the left.

Not phoning could cost you the whole deal. So pick up the phone. Then watch your business pick up.

BUSINESS HOURS*				
Continental European Time	American Working Hours			
	Eastern	Central	Mountain	Pacific
3 P.M.	9 A.M.			
4 P.M.	10 A.M.	9 A.M.		
5 P.M.	11 A.M.	10 A.M.	9 A.M.	
6 P.M.	12 P.M.	11 A.M.	10 A.M.	9 A.M.
7 P.M.	1 P.M.	12 P.M.	11 A.M.	10 A.M.
8 P.M.	2 P.M.	1 P.M.	12 P.M.	11 A.M.
9 P.M.	3 P.M.	2 P.M.	1 P.M.	12 P.M.
10 P.M.	4 P.M.	3 P.M.	2 P.M.	1 P.M.
11 P.M.	5 P.M.	4 P.M.	3 P.M.	2 P.M.

*Based on 6 hours time difference. (Time difference may be more or less, depending on country and season.)

 **Bell System**

A Look at these sections before you read the text:

1 VOCABULARY

wheels of Brie pieces of Brie cheese shaped like a wheel
on hand available now
on the line on the telephone
right on the spot immediately
(to) close the deal (to) agree to the details of the deal
schedule table; chart; list
watch your business pick up your business will improve

Now read the text and answer the skim questions.

2 SKIM

a What is the advertisement selling?
b How can you find out when Americans are at work?

B Look at these sections after reading the text:

3 COMPREHENSION

a What does Norm want to buy?
b Why will it cost more than he expects?
c What is the deal the two men make?
d What is the earliest time you can call an American in central USA from Europe, if you want to find him in the office?
e Why does a telephone conversation help to make a deal?

4 INFERENCE

a How could 'not phoning cost you the whole deal'?
b How does a two-way conversation get questions answered?
c Why do Americans like to do business on the phone? What difference does it make?

5 REFERENCE

a What is Brie, and where does it come from?
b What is Feta, and where does it come from?
c Explain what Eastern, Central, Mountain and Pacific are. Where are they?
d What is the Bell System?

6 LANGUAGE

Look at these sentences from the text:
  *Americans like to **do** business by phone.*
  *So **make** it your business to talk it over....*
Make and *do* give different meanings to the sentences. Try to find the right word for these sentences—use either *make* or *do*.
a In business it is important to . . . . . . contacts.
b You won't be successful if you don't . . . . . . any work.
c . . . . . . me a favour—check this report for me.
d Packaging doesn't really . . . . . . any difference to the product.
e . . . . . . it right—don't . . . . . . a mess of this project.

7 OPINION

a Bell is an American telephone company. Why does Bell want Europeans to call America? Any Europeans calling America will not pay Bell for the telephone calls, but their own national company.
b What image of American business does this advertisement give? Is it an accurate picture, in your opinion?
c What do you think of the style of the conversation in the picture? Is it polite, formal, friendly, informal, rude? What do you think? What does it tell you about the people?
d Do you think your business would improve if you telephoned the USA more often? How could this help some businesses?

8 WRITING

a You are Norm. Write a letter confirming your order, and confirming the deal you have made.
b Write a short memo for your European colleagues, explaining when they can find American businesspeople in their offices. Explain the system for New York, Chicago, Denver and Los Angeles.
c Write to Bell asking for the prices of calls to America from your country.

TIME B.

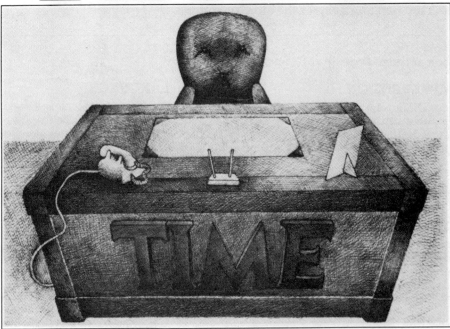

What to do if Business Week takes your advertising to the right kind of people, but not enough of them.

Chances are that if you think about advertising to businessmen you think of traditional business magazines—and with good reason.

But there's another way to talk business to business people. Possibly an even better way.

TIME B (for Business). It's the advertising edition of TIME Magazine directed *exclusively* to businessmen...businessmen qualified by both job title and industry. And TIME B circulates solely in the United States.

It's the largest all-business circulation you can buy: 1,550,000. And at the most efficient price: almost five dollars per thousand less than you get through Business Week.

But is TIME B really a business publication? No, frankly it's not that limited. It satisfies the businessman's hunger to understand the world in which he *lives* as well as works: it lets him touch on art, humanities, and science; books, politics, and law.

To you, they're businessmen. But TIME talks to them as people. And interests them profoundly. Try TIME B. It's *more* than just another business publication.

Circulation:	1,550,000	Average Household Income:	$50,900
B&W Page Rate:	$24,585	Attended College:	87.5%
4-Color Page Rate:	$38,350	Professional/Managerial:	100%

1979 estimate; updated by Data Research Company.

There's a right TIME for every advertiser.

A Look at these sections before you read the text:

1 VOCABULARY

chances are it is likely that
exclusively only
solely only
frankly to be honest
(to) touch on (to) deal with; (to) be involved with
profoundly deeply

Now read the text and answer the skim questions.

2 SKIM

a What is this text advertising?
b Who is the text aimed at?
c Where was this text published?

B Look at these sections after reading the text:

3 COMPREHENSION

a What is *Time B*?
b How is it different from *Time* magazine?
c Why is it better than *Business Week*?
d What is *Business Week*? How do we know?

4 INFERENCE

a What does '5 dollars per thousand' mean? Per thousand what?
b What do the statistics prove? What is their purpose?
c Where is *Business Week* sold? Is it different from *Time B*?
d Why is it important that 87.5% of *Time B*'s readers went to college?

5 REFERENCE

a What is B&W?
b What is the 'page rate'?

6 LANGUAGE

Look at this phrase from the text:
    . . . *interests them profoundly* . . .
Another way of saying this is:
    . . . *they have a profound interest* . . .
Change these sentences in the same way:
a He reported the trends precisely. It was a . . . . . .
b He studied the market carefully. It was a . . . . . .
c The committee met regularly. They had a . . . . . .
d They decided unanimously. It was a . . . . . .
e The firm was organised hierarchically. It had a . . . . . .

7 OPINION

a What do you think is the meaning of the picture?
b The advertisement suggests that *Business Week* is not as good as *Time B*. Do you think it is fair for advertisers to criticise other companies? Should this be allowed? Is it allowed in your country?
c *Time B* says it is better because it gives not only business news, but science, art, politics and so on as well. What sort of magazine would you prefer? Only business news, or a mixture like *Time B*?
d *Time B* is only sold in the United States. Why do you think it is not sold in other countries?

8 WRITING

a Write a report for your Marketing Manager, explaining the statistics given here. Advise him which magazine he should place your advertisements in.
b Imagine you work for *Business Week* magazine. Write an advertisement to answer this one from *Time B*. Be unfair if you want to!

These labels are mixed up.
Are you?

The Problem:

Three boxes are labeled "Apples", "Oranges", and "Apples and Oranges". Each label is incorrect. How can you relabel each box correctly by looking at only one piece of fruit from one box?

Only a fruit picked from the "Apples and Oranges" box guarantees a correct answer. If you choose an apple you know it must be only apples. Therefore the box marked "Apples" must be oranges and the box marked "Oranges" must be apples and oranges. Likewise, an orange picked from the "Apples and Oranges" box is conclusive.

The Solution:

The right first move is the key to solving most problems.

If the right first move on the puzzle above has you stumped, look in the back of this magazine under *Creative Problem Solving.* ✳ But if you are searching for the answer to a production problem, the right first move may be a call to FMC.

Our Engineered Systems Division is uniquely qualified at analyzing tough production problems, then designing and building the special machines or machinery systems that solve the problem.

If you need to increase throughput, lower unit cost or bring a new product from prototype to production we can help make your next move the right move.

FMC has offices across the U.S. To find out more or to talk over a problem, call us at (800) 538-6858/CA (408) 280-9000.

FMC Corporation, Engineered Systems Division, 328 Brokaw Rd., Santa Clara, CA 95052.

A Look at these sections before you read the text:

1 VOCABULARY

label name or title on a container
stumped confused
throughput amount of work going through the system
prototype first example of a new product

Now read the text and answer the skim questions.

2 SKIM

a What is the advertisement trying to sell?
b What have apples and oranges got to do with business?

B Look at these sections after reading the text:

3 COMPREHENSION

a What problems can FMC solve?
b What does their Engineered Systems Division do for the customers?
c What is the best way to solve any problem, according to FMC?

4 INFERENCE

a Why could the 'right first move' in solving a problem be a call to FMC?
b What is the connection between solving the problem in the picture, and solving a business problem?

5 REFERENCE

a What does CA refer to in the address of FMC?
b Why are there different telephone numbers, with different codes, but only one address? Find out what the (800) code refers to.

6 LANGUAGE

The expression 'mixed up' has two meanings, one literal and one figurative. Find them out and describe the two meanings in sentences.

Do the same for these words from the text:
    key move stumped

7 OPINION

a What do you think is the answer to the problem described here? What box would you look in?
b Why do you think the advertisers chose this idea for the FMC advertisement? What do they want you to think about FMC?

8 WRITING

a Your company has a production problem—it wants to speed up production without taking on more workers. Imagine you are telephoning FMC for help. Write down your conversation.
b Imagine there is a prize for getting the correct answer to the puzzle. Write out the correct way to solve it. Use an impersonal style, as you would for a company report: *The first thing to be done is. . . .*

*N.B. The answer is now printed upside down under the problem.

What to Buy
for business

11 Kings Road
London SW3 4RP
Tel: 01-730 0405

TJB/viw

15th May 19..

Dear Sir

Following our recent trial offer of <u>What to Buy</u>, we are currently updating our
subscription records.

You should by now have received three free issues of <u>What to Buy</u>, and a pro forma
invoice. The April edition (covering copiers, overseas deliveries and office cleaning)
is now available, and in order for our subscriptions department to know whether to
put you on their list for this and future ediitons, it would be appreciated if vou
would return the enclosed prepaid card if you wish to subscribe.

If you do not return the card, it will be assumed that you do not wish to continue
receiving <u>What to Buy</u>, and you will be sent no reminders.

There is no need to send payment with the reply card: simply settle the pro forma
invoice in due course.

We hope that whether or not you are continuing with <u>What to Buy</u>, the three issues
you have seen have been useful.

Yours faithfully

Tracey Baines

<u>TRACEY BAINES</u>

Enc.

P.S. If you have already indicated
      that you are subscribing by
      settling the pro forma invoice,
      please ignore this letter and
      the reply card.

 The independent monthly report on business equipment and services
An Oppenheim Derrick publication

Reproduced by kind permission of *What to buy for business* magazine.

A Look at these sections before you read the text:

1 VOCABULARY

trial offer introduction to the product
updating bringing up-to-date
pro forma invoice an invoice to be paid before goods
are delivered
covering describing; dealing with
prepaid postage paid by us
in due course at some future time, soon; when
appropriate
yours faithfully letter-ending when you do not know
the name of the receiver of the letter

Now read the text and answer the skim questions.

2 SKIM

a Why has the magazine sent this letter?
b What action should the receiver of the letter take?

B Look at these sections after reading the text:

3 COMPREHENSION

a What has the magazine already sent to you (the
receiver of the letter)?
b Why did they send you anything?
c What do they want you to do now?
d What will happen if you do not reply to the letter?
e If you have already bought a subscription, what should
you do?

4 INFERENCE

a Why should the magazine give away three free copies
of the publication? What does this suggest about the
magazine?
b Why are they referring to the April magazine,
although the letter is dated May?
c Why should they provide the reader with free
postage?

5 REFERENCE

a What is a pro forma invoice and why is it used?
b What is 'copier' an abbreviation of?

6 LANGUAGE

Look at this sentence from the text:
   If you do not return the card, it will be assumed that . . .
This is the form of an *if*-sentence, which explains the
consequences of an action. Finish these *if*-sentences by
adding the consequence of the action:

a If you don't send us payment, we . . . . . .
b If you pay the invoice, we . . . . . .
c If the magazine gets no new subscribers, it . . . . . .
d If you write a letter to the magazine, they . . . . . .
e If the magazine's writers think a new product is very
bad, they . . . . . .

7 OPINION

a What does the magazine write about? What sort of
readers does it want?
b Can you find the typing error? What is it? What
impression does it make when you find mistakes in a
business letter?
c Do you think there is a need for a magazine that
reports on different types of business equipment?
What would you expect from such a magazine?
d In what way do you think it is independent?

8 WRITING

a Write a reply to the letter, explaining why you do (or
do not) want to subscribe to the magazine.
b Choose an area of business equipment that you know
well, and write a report on the best types of
equipment, the possible problems with the
equipment, comparison of prices, and so on.

It takes more than grapes to make a vintage wine.

It takes a quality glass container.

In fact, fine wine develops its character in the bottle. And O-I is the leading producer of glass for America's flourishing wine

We'll never run short of the raw materials used to make glass.

industry. (Wine consumption in the U.S. has increased 67% in just ten years.)

Glass is Class

No other package makes sense for fine wine. Or for other products that must project an image of *class*.

No other form of packaging delivers so much good taste at such a low cost. Or is made from such abundant, domestic natural resources as sand, soda ash and limestone.

Small wonder glass is also today's fastest-growing package for food and beverages.

The Creative Container

At O-I, we keep finding ways to innovate with glass.

Consider our Plasti-Shield™ container.

Its foam-insulated jacket takes color printing beautifully. Which makes it a natural for the best-selling brands of soft drinks, mouthwash, juices, fruit drinks and pre-mixed cocktails.

Beer is going great in glass bottles, too. Bottle shipments were up 7% last year — to more than 16 billion containers. As Chris Schenkel says for us on TV and radio, "The Good Taste of Beer Comes in a Bottle."

Everything looks great in O-I glass. And we have the latest twists in closures, too.

Libbey® Leads in Glassware

Glass shows its class on your table, too. Our Libbey Glass Division creates hundreds of popular priced ideas every year in home and institutional glassware.

In 1979, Libbey introduced some 315 new styles, shapes and decorations. So it's

Libbey is the word for innovation in glassware — at home and away.

not surprising that surveys continue to identify Libbey as the best known name in table glassware.

Glass. It's the 2,000-year-old vintage idea in packaging. At O-I, we're making it newer every year.

We have what it takes.

O-I

OWENS-ILLINOIS

Toledo, Ohio 43666

A Look at these sections before you read the text:

1 VOCABULARY

vintage the year a wine is made; if it's a good vintage, it's a good wine
flourishing growing successfully
consumption the use of a product; *here*, how much wine is drunk
abundant there is a lot of this material
domestic at home; *here*, available in the USA
limestone type of rock
small wonder it's not surprising

2 SKIM

a What product is this advertisement selling? Or is it a service?
b What does Libbey produce?

Now read the text and answer the skim questions.

B Look at these sections after reading the text:

3 COMPREHENSION

a What is glass made of?
b What is a Plasti-Shield container?
c Why is glass a better form of packaging?
d What sort of glass does Libbey produce?

4 INFERENCE

a Why is it important what 'image' a container projects?
b Whose surveys show that Libbey is the best-known name in glass? Who pays for these surveys?
c Why is it mentioned that glass is made from *domestic* natural resources?

5 REFERENCE

a What is soda ash?
b Who is Chris Schenkel?
c What is a pre-mixed cocktail?

6 LANGUAGE

Look at this sentence from the text:
> . . . *is made from such abundant domestic natural resources* . . .

The adjective *abundant* comes before *domestic*. *Domestic* is the more definite, the more factual description of the natural resources. *Abundant* is more a matter of opinion, and so it comes earlier. It is usual for adjectives to be positioned in this order. Try to put the adjectives in the right order in these sentences:

a This furniture is in the. . . . . .style. (American, early)
b We live in a. . . . . .house. (huge, old)
c He's a very. . . . . .man. (young, clever)
d It's a. . . . . .day today. (beautiful, sunny)

7 OPINION

a Why do you think wine consumption has increased by 67% in the last 10 years?
b Does beer (or wine) really taste better in a glass? Does the type of container make any difference to the taste of the drink?
c Surveys show that Libbey is the best-known name in glass. Do you think this means it is the best quality producer? Would you buy their products because the name is well-known?
d Do you think packaging is important? What effect does it have on people?

8 WRITING

a Imagine you work for Owens-Illinois. How would you write an advertisement to persuade people to buy glass? Write a text for a newspaper advertisement.
b You work for a beer company. Your boss wants to put the beer in cans, because it's cheaper. Write a memo explaining why glass is better, despite the extra cost.

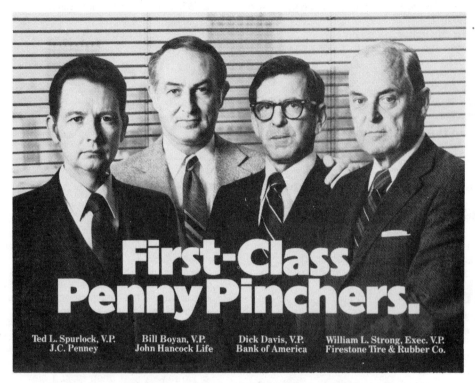

Ted L. Spurlock, V.P.   Bill Boyan, V.P.   Dick Davis, V.P.   William L. Strong, Exec. V.P.
J.C. Penney   John Hancock Life   Bank of America   Firestone Tire & Rubber Co.

Last year, with Presort™, they pinched more than $2,000,000 off their First-Class postage costs.

Pinching pennies isn't a glamorous job. It's just good business. And last year, some very good business people – more than 15,000 across the country – saved themselves a small fortune on their First-Class mailing costs. Two little pennies at a time.

You sort, you save.

Using Presort is simple: before you bring your First-Class Mail to the Post Office, you presort it by ZIP Code according to simple regulations. That saves us some valuable time. And, for that time, we give you a 2¢ lower rate on every First-Class letter and a 1¢ lower rate on each postcard. It may not sound like much, but as these people and thousands of other Presort users will attest, it certainly adds up.

Who uses Presort?

If your company has at least 500 First-Class Mail pieces per mailing, you're Presort material.

Setting Presort up.

Depending on the mail volume, each Presort System is tailored for your particular business. A Customer Service Representative will visit your mail facility, evaluate your needs and even aid you in setting your system up.

So become a First-Class Penny Pincher. Just send in the coupon below for details or give your local Postmaster a call. Where else can you pinch that many pennies and still go First-Class?

PRESORT™
CUTS THE COST OF FIRST-CLASS MAIL

© USPS 1980

To: Asst. Postmaster General, Customer Svcs.
U.S. Postal Service, Room 5676 AG-2
475 L'Enfant Plaza West, S.W.
Washington, D.C. 20260

U.S. POSTAL SERVICE ®

Please send Presort literature to:

Name _____

Company _____

Street _____

City _____ State _____ ZIP _____

Annual Mail Volume:
(Check one)
☐ 100,000 pieces or less
☐ 100,000 – 1,000,000 pieces
☐ 1,000,000 and above

Type of Business: (Check one)
☐ Banking   ☐ Retail
☐ Education   ☐ Medical
☐ Government   ☐ Manufacturing
☐ Publishing   ☐ Other

A Look at these sections before you read the text:

1 VOCABULARY

penny US 1 cent; GB 1p
penny pincher a mean person, a person who does not like to spend money unnecessarily
(to) pinch (to) squeeze; *here*, (to) save
tailored designed for you
(to) attest (to) give evidence
setting . . . up starting

2 SKIM

a Who organises Presort?
b How can it save money for a company?

Now read the text and answer the skim questions.

B Look at these sections after reading the text:

3 COMPREHENSION

a What exactly is presorting? Who does it?
b How much can you save?
c What condition is there? What makes it possible for you to use this system?
d What does the representative do for you?

4 INFERENCE

a What is first-class postage? What does this tell you about the US postage system?
b Why is this lower price offered? What is the advantage for the postal service?
c What is the purpose of the photo of the four company men? Why are they in the advertisement?

5 REFERENCE

a What does V.P. refer to in the names of the men pictured?
b Find out what a ZIP code is.
c In the address coupon there are several abbreviations. Find out the meaning of the following:
Asst.   Svcs.   D.C.

6 LANGUAGE

Look at these sentences from the text:
Pinching pennies isn't a glamorous job.
Using Presort is simple.
These are more interesting ways of saying:
It isn't glamorous to pinch pennies.
It's simple to use Presort.
Now make these sentences more interesting in the same way:
a It's good business to save postage costs.
b It doesn't take long to presort the first-class mail.
c The job of the Customer Service Representative is to set your system up.
d In this economic climate it's important to cut costs where possible.
e It makes sense for the Postal Service to reduce sorting time with this scheme.

7 OPINION

a Do you think this is a good way of saving money? Would it be cheaper to pay someone in the company to presort the letters, rather than charge lower postage? How can you work this out?
b The text mentions 'simple regulations' which tell you how the mail should be sorted. What could these be? What do you think will be necessary?

8 WRITING

a Write a letter to the US Postal Service explaining the sort of mail your company sends, and asking for further details of how you can save money.
b You are the executive in charge of a company programme to cut costs. Write a report for your boss giving the pros and cons of this scheme, and what you think the company should do about it.

Now there's something from Philips that makes work much easier for the secretary, the boss and even the head of a small firm.

It's the Philips Micro-Computer P 2000.

This is how it works:

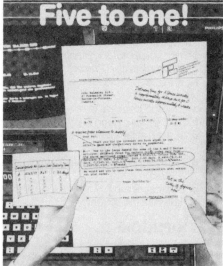

Five to one! One o'clock!

"You always want it at the last minute!" How many times have you heard that from your secretary? But the most important things are often the last minute things. And that's where you want to save time. Time that costs money.

The Philips P 2000 Micro-Computer helps you to deal with all sorts of work quickly and efficiently.

Anyone who can use an electric typewriter can operate the Philips P 2000. It's as simple as that. What's more, you'll be agreeably surprised by its reasonable price!

Simplicity and versatility – that's what makes the P 2000 ideal for the small business. Even if you only use the P 2000 for correspondence, it pays for itself. Letters

needing correction don't have to be fully retyped – simply call up the stored text on the screen and type corrections in.

You can change text easily, turn it around or add or delete whole paragraphs. The new correct letter appears on the screen instantly. Touch a key and as many originals as you like are typed out. And stored rou-

tine letters are typed out automatically.

But this is only a fraction of what the P 2000 can do. It can do much, much more. Bookkeeping, invoicing, statistics and record systems.

So the P 2000 offers you everything you need for a small business or as a self-employed professional. A total computer service that you can quickly and easily put to use

in all areas of your business.

And behind all this, naturally, is the Philips name. The name that stands for experience and first class service.

 Data Systems

Please send me complete information on the Philips Micro-Computer P 2000

Name

Address

Philips Business Equipment. (P 2000), Mullard House, Torrington Place, London WC1E 7HD

Philips Austria (P 2000). Triester Strasse 64, A-1100 Vienna

Philips Micro-Computer

P2000

Simply for everyone.

PHILIPS

A Look at these sections before you read the text:

1 VOCABULARY

five to one 12.55
agreeably pleasantly
reasonable cheap; not too expensive
versatility ability to do different jobs
stored (material) kept in the memory
(to) delete (to) get rid of; (to) take out
fraction very small part

Now read the text and answer the skim questions.

2 SKIM

a Who is this product designed for?
b What can it do? Find two types of work it can do.

B Look at these sections after reading the text:

3 COMPREHENSION

a What is 'surprising' about the P 2000?
b How can it make letter-writing faster?
c How can you change texts with the P 2000?

4 INFERENCE

a What is the meaning of the two pictures and the two times?
b The title suggests that this computer can work for many different sorts of people. What makes it useful for everybody?
c The advertisement refers to 'the Philips name'—what are the readers supposed to think of when they think of Philips?

5 LANGUAGE

Look at this sentence from the text:
Letters needing correction don't have to be retyped.
This is another way of saying:
Letters which need correction . . .
Rewrite these sentences in the same way:
a The staff who need training in the use of the computer should see the manager.
b The train which leaves at 10.30 is for Amsterdam.
c Computers which require maintenance must be returned to Philips.
d Anyone who takes a free day without permission will be sacked.

6 OPINION

a Do you think computers are a good idea in offices? Do they save work, or only create more work?
b Is this machine really a computer, or just a word-processor? Is it trying to be both machines? If so, is that a good idea?
c Are there any disadvantages in writing letters or doing the accounts and so on on a computer or word-processor? What must you be very careful about?

7 WRITING

a Write to Philips and ask for more details on the price, delivery time, servicing and so on of the P 2000.
b Write a memo to your boss explaining why you think you (or your secretary) should get a word-processor or computer.

---

bacie bridging the information gap

I need to be aware of national events affecting my work in the education and training fields. How can you help?

News Service: Written by the information staff using material abstracted from press releases, reports, conferences and relevant contacts, the News and Comment pages of the BACIE Journal give details of government, educational and industrial activities in these fields. The library maintains a file of press cuttings.

Your training

problem?

How can I best present my training programme?

Training Aids: BACIE's information officers can supply you with details of audio-visual hardware and software, including boards, projectors, training packages, business games, video equipment, simulators and accessories. If you want a film, filmstrip or video programme we can suggest titles and provide producers' addresses. An illustrated Training Aids Page in the BACIE Journal keeps members informed of media developments.

I would like to improve my knowledge of interpersonal skills. Have you any books on the subject?

Library: BACIE has a library which contains over 4500 books about most aspects of vocational education and training. The lending service, available to UK members, is free of charge. Visitors are always welcome to use the library for reference. Members are kept informed of new publications added to stock through the BACIE Bibliography, a quarterly supplement to the BACIE Journal.

I want to inform my staff about employment legislation. How can I find out about all the relevant books, visual aids, packages and courses?

Information Summaries: We produce, on request, summaries of material on a particular subject: books and articles, courses, training aids on the subject, including all relevant addresses.

Our training officer saw an article about individualised instruction in a journal last month and I would like a copy. Can you help?

Information Extracts: We can provide you with articles and information abstracted from journals and newspapers. This material is available on loan. For individual private use photocopies may be made for a small charge.

I need a conference centre in Surrey which can accommodate 16 people for four days.

Conference Venues: When you need information about training centres or hotels with conference facilities available for hire, the department can supply lists of hotel and centre names and addresses on request.

Where can I send my secretary to acquire better understanding of the manager's role?

Courses and Conferences: The department can supply information on dates, location, content and costs from its collection of directories, leaflets and prospectuses.

The services indicated above have been developed in response to members' information needs. Please let us know if any additional information service would be helpful to you.

A Look at these sections before you read the text:

1 VOCABULARY

(to) bridge the gap (to) do something that is needed; (to) remedy a deficiency

abstracted summarised

press cuttings articles from newspapers and magazines

vocational training training for work, for a career

quarterly every three months

(to) acquire (to) get; (to) obtain

prospectus information sheet or booklet

Now read the text and answer the skim questions.

2 SKIM

a What does BACIE do?

b What area of the business world does it specialise in?

B Look at these sections after reading the text:

3 COMPREHENSION

a Who is allowed to take books out of the library? How much does it cost?

b How do people find out about new books in the library?

c What is the title of the people who work in BACIE?

d How can BACIE help you with conference organisation?

4 INFERENCE

a What do the letters B.A.C.I.E. mean?

b What is the BACIE journal, and how often is it published?

c What are the implications of the design? Are all the services available by telephone?

5 REFERENCE

a What country is BACIE in? How do you know? Does this help to explain what B.A.C.I.E. means?

b What is 'Surrey' and where is it?

6 LANGUAGE

Look at this sentence from the text:
Written by the information staff. . ., the pages of the BACIE Journal. . . give details.
This is a combination of two sentences:
The pages of the BACIE Journal give details. . .
The pages of the BACIE Journal are written by the information staff. . .
Now join these pairs of sentences together in the same way. Start the sentence with the word in italics:

a The BACIE bibliography is *published* regularly.
The BACIE bibliography keeps members informed of new books.

b Information summaries provide notes and addresses on a specific subject.
Information summaries are *produced* on request.

c BACIE is *supported* by members' subscriptions.
BACIE tries to provide information at low cost.

7 OPINION

a Would this information service be useful for your company? What sort of information do you need most often?

b There is no address on this information sheet—so how could you find out more information about BACIE?

c Would your company be prepared to send people overseas (to BACIE) for training or for conferences? Is training considered very important? Does your company use the training films, videos, management games and so on that BACIE offers?

8 WRITING

a Write a short letter to BACIE asking how you can become a member, and how much it costs.

b Write a note to the Training Manager of your company, asking if he knows about BACIE and if he would be interested in more information.

The Bell System CREDIT CARD

When you're away from home on business or vacation travel, making a simple Long Distance call is not always simple. Not enough change. Operators interrupting your conversation while you fumble for another coin.

Forget it. And speed your Long Distance calling with a handy Bell System Credit Card. It's free, convenient, and your calls will cost no more than any other operator-assisted call.

There's more. Besides the freedom to call from anywhere to anywhere else at any time, you don't pay for your calls until your next regular bill arrives. Credit Card calls will be listed separately for a precise record of your Credit Card charges.

When you travel abroad, your Bell System Credit Card helps you avoid the extremely high surcharges that many foreign hotels add to International calls. And your credit card is honored from any phone in the United States, Canada, more than 100 foreign countries—even ships at sea—on calls back to the United States.

There's *no additional charge* for the added convenience of a Bell System Credit Card. Just fill out the attached postage-free application, tear it off, and mail it today. Or if you prefer, leave the card attached, fold the cover side in (so our address shows on the outside) and staple or tape closed. If you qualify for a Bell System Credit Card, it will arrive in 6-8 weeks.

If you already have a Bell System Credit Card, it is not necessary to complete this application. Annual renewal is automatic.

(PLEASE TYPE OR PRINT)

I authorize C&P Telephone to issue _____ Bell System Telephone Credit Card(s) in my name.
Please Note: Credit Cards are issued in billing name only.

_____
Billing Name

_____
Billing Street Address

_____
Billing City, State, Zip Code

Bill all charges for calls made with this card or cards to my **RESIDENCE** Telephone number listed below:

_____
Area code   **RESIDENCE** Telephone number

I understand that the Bell System Telephone Credit Card is service extended to C&P Telephone customers and that my account will be reviewed before I am issued a card.

_____   _____
Please sign in ink   Date

This Bell System Telephone Credit Card application is for C&P Telephone customers only.

(7/80, 8/80, 9/80)

A Look at these sections before you read the text:

1 VOCABULARY

(to) fumble (to) search for something, clumsily
handy easy to use; convenient; useful
surcharge extra charge
(to) staple (to) fix with a short metal pin (usually through paper)
annual every year
(to) authorise (to) give permission to someone

2 SKIM

a What is the purpose of the application form?
b What must you do to get the service?

Now read the text and answer the skim questions.

B Look at these sections after reading the text:

3 COMPREHENSION

a How much does the credit card service cost?
b Where can you use the card?
c How can you get it?
d How long will it take to get a card?
e Who is this service for? Can everybody use it?

4 INFERENCE

a How does the card work? How do you make telephone calls with it?
b How long does the card last?
c Can you use it to call from England to Italy? How?/Why not?

5 REFERENCE

a What is C&P? What do the letters C and P mean?
b What is a Zip Code?
c What is an Area Code?

6 LANGUAGE

Look at this sentence from the text:
When you're away from home on business or vacation travel. . .
Vacation is an American word. British speakers would use the word *holiday*. Try to find the American words in the text which mean the same as these British English words:
a fill in
b post
c postcode
d dialling code
e trunk calling
f name of the person paying the bills

7 OPINION

a What do you think are the advantages of a telephone credit card? Are there any disadvantages?
b Why do you think that an account 'will be reviewed' before a card is issued? Why does the company do this?
c The card takes about 6–8 weeks to arrive. Why do you think it takes so long?

8 WRITING

a Write a memo to your boss explaining what the Bell System Credit Card is, and why you think the company should give you one.
b Write a short letter to C&P Telephone, explaining that you are not yet a C&P customer, but you would like a Bell System card. Ask whether this can be arranged.

PUBLISHERS FOR THE ROYAL NETHERLANDS ACADEMY OF ARTS AND SCIENCES

NORTH-HOLLAND PUBLISHING COMPANY
(B.V. NOORD-HOLLANDSCHE UITGEVERSMAATSCHAPPIJ)

MOLENWERF 1, P.O. BOX 211, 1000 AE AMSTERDAM, THE NETHERLANDS, TELEPHONE (020) 58039 11

June, 19 . .

Dear Sir/Madam,

It is with great pleasure that North-Holland Publishing Company hereby presents the first issue of its new journal MATERIALS LETTERS.

The aim of this journal is to reach and provide a forum for scientists and engineers trained in the traditional disciplines of chemistry, physics, ceramics and metallurgy, now engaged in the interdisciplinary field of the science and technology of materials.

Our market research has shown that there is a need for a channel that allows rapid publication of short papers on various aspects of the field in order to stimulate its further development and to encourage the cross-fertilization of ideas from scientists with a variety of backgrounds. We firmly believe that this interdisciplinary Letters Journal will be a valuable and necessary addition to the materials research literature.

As your library already subscribes to at least one of the materials related periodicals published by us, we have developed the following scheme for you: Volume 1 (1982) will be mailed to you FREE OF CHARGE. The only thing we ask from you is to display the issues prominently in the appropriate section of your library, so that they are easily accessible to the interested research workers. Should you require additional copies of the first issue for internal circulation, please let me know. They are available!

In 1983 Volume 2 in 6 issues will be published. Subscription price, postage and handling included, will be Dfl.220.00/US$88.00. (Dfl. price is definitive).

Please make sure that information on MATERIALS LETTERS is entered into your administrative system, since this will inform your library users of its existence and availability.

For additional information, please contact the undersigned.

Yours sincerely,

Ms. C. Schilpp
Marketing Manager

Enc

Cables: NOHUM AMSTERDAM, Telex: 18582 ESPA NL
Commercial Register nr. 39854

A Look at these sections before you read the text:

1 VOCABULARY

hereby by this means; in this way
forum a place to discuss
engaged in involved in; busy with
interdisciplinary involving two or more types of
science or other academic subject
channel method of communication
crossfertilisation influence of one idea on another idea
periodicals magazines
definitive most important; it leads the others
the undersigned the person who signed this letter

Now read the text and answer the skim questions.

2 SKIM

a What sort of magazine is *Materials Letters*?
b What is the special offer the company is making?

B Look at these sections after reading the text:

3 COMPREHENSION

a What sort of people would want to read this journal?
b In what way is it different from other journals in the field?
c How did North-Holland get the address of the company who received this letter?
d What must you do if you want a free copy of the first volume of the journal?
e How much does one issue of the journal cost?

4 INFERENCE

a Why does the publishing company want to give one year's subscription of the journal free? This offer comes at the end of the publishing year—Volume 1 has already been published. What does this suggest about the journal?
b Why is there an emphasis on the *rapid* publication of short papers? What does this suggest about this type of journal?
c Why does the letter say 'Dfl. price is definitive' after the prices are given?

5 REFERENCE

a The letters 'Dfl.' have two references—one to the thing they describe, and one to the words that begin with 'd' 'f' or 'l'. Explain the references.

6 LANGUAGE

Look at this sentence from the text:
> It is with great pleasure that North-Holland Publishing Company hereby presents the first issue of . . .

This is a very formal way of saying:
> We are happy to present the first issue of . . .

Find the *formal* words or phrases used in the text which mean:
a suitable
b extra
c where it can be seen
d easily found
e journals about materials research

7 OPINION

a The letter suggests that journals for scientists often publish the papers sent to them only after a long delay. Why is it so difficult to publish the papers quickly?
b How do you think the company found out that scientists wanted papers published quickly? What market research methods would you use in this situation?
c Since this journal is for specialists and scientists, it will be of interest only to these people. If they are serious about their speciality, they will get the specialist journals anyway. Do you think it is necessary to advertise and use special marketing offers like this?
d Do you think this is a profit-making company, or a public service company?

8 WRITING

a Write a note to your colleague in charge of the company library. Explain what this new journal is about, and what the special offer is.
b Imagine you are producing a new journal in your specialist field, and you want to send out a letter like this in order to get more customers. Write a letter giving details of your own special offer.

FACTORING SUCCESS   1

Peter Muss (right), with company secretary, Brian Alexander, outside Hyscot's new factory.

'To us, it simply means growth'

To say that factoring can have a dramatic effect on a company's growth is an understatement.

Ask Peter Muss, managing director of Hydraulic Cranes (Scotland), the company he founded at Blackwood, Strathclyde eight years ago.

'The closer we looked at factoring, the more we liked it. We believed that with a dynamic sales team we needed dynamic financial backing, and we've certainly got that with Alex Lawrie Factors', says Peter.

Hydraulic Cranes – or Hyscot for short – began operating in 1971. Within a few months it had taken over a second company, Hydraulic Breakers.

Peter Muss had recognised the importance of the market for hydraulic-powered tools, and his company is now a leading maker of this type of equipment in the North, with a turnover this year of £2 million.

Hydraulic Cranes (Scotland), started factoring quite recently, and hasn't looked back.

'We'd got to the point in 1978 where we couldn't get satisfactory financial backing to support our rapid growth, without giving away equity for working capital, or without losing control of the company altogether', says Mr. Muss.

'We chose to link up with Alex Lawrie Factors, because of the very fast response and assistance provided by their Scottish Manager. Once we started factoring, the improvement in the situation was very quickly felt.'

It's a simple operation. The company sends all its sales invoices to Alex Lawrie, who send them to the customers. Next day, it receives 70% of their value, minus a service charge. The remaining 30%, less any interest charge, is passed on as soon as the invoices have been paid.

'Our sales directors are now given free rein to sell as much as possible, with the assurance that the debtors can quickly be exchanged for cash.'

⛵ Alex Lawrie Factors

Alex Lawrie Factors Limited, Reform Club, Warwick Row, Coventry CV1 1EX

A Look at these sections before you read the text:

1 VOCABULARY

factoring a type of credit; another company pays you the money your customers owe you
understatement saying something is less important than it really is
hydraulic operated by the force of water
backing support; help
turnover total gross sales
equity ownership rights
free rein freedom; independence

Now read the text and answer the skim questions.

2 SKIM

a Find out about factoring: what percentage of your unpaid invoices do you get?
b Where is the Hyscot company based?

B Look at these sections after reading the text:

3 COMPREHENSION

a Who are the men in the photograph? What do they think about factoring?
b What exactly happens when you use a factoring company? What must you do?
c Why did Hyscot start factoring? What were their alternatives?
d Why did they choose to work with Alex Lawrie Factors?

4 INFERENCE

a Why did Hyscot think factoring was better than giving up some equity? What are the advantages of keeping all the equity?
b What are the full costs of factoring? What percentage of your invoices do you lose? Are all the costs explained here?
c Peter Muss talks of 'improvement' after he began factoring. What sort of improvement could this be?

5 REFERENCE

a What is Strathclyde?
b Brian Alexander is the company secretary of Hyscot. What are his responsibilities in the company?

6 LANGUAGE

Look at this sentence from the text:
  'Once we started factoring, the improvement in the situation was very quickly felt.'
If you wanted to report this sentence from Peter Muss, you would say:
  Peter Muss said that once he had started factoring, the improvement in the situation had been very quickly felt.
Now report these sentences from Mr Muss in the same way:
a 'The closer we looked at factoring, the more we liked it.'
b 'We chose to link up with Alex Lawrie Factors, because they were helpful.'
c 'We have had three good years with Alex Lawrie, who have been very helpful.'

7 OPINION

a Do you think factoring is a good idea? Why?/Why not?
b Do you think factoring is more or less expensive than borrowing money from a bank? In what way is it different from borrowing from a bank?
c Would you recommend factoring as a way of getting more money for your business? Why?/Why not?
d What are the possible risks in factoring, for the company and for the factoring company?

8 WRITING

a Write to Peter Muss of Hyscot, asking him for his advice on factoring. Ask him if he has had any problems with this service.
b Imagine you work for Alex Lawrie. A potential customer has written to you asking for more information on factoring. Write a reply, explaining how factoring works and why it would be useful to him.

**Business
Traveller**
the travel magazine

60/61 Fleet Street,
London EC4Y 1LA England.
Tel: 01-583-0967
Telex 8814624 EXPTMS

BB

Dear Traveller,

DID YOU PAY TOO MUCH FOR YOUR LAST INTERNATIONAL BUSINESS TRIP?

"You can travel economy class around the world with confirmed
reservations stopping over in Hong-Kong, Tokyo, Honolulu, Los
Angeles, New York and London for only £550 - if you know which
fares to ask for ...."

"You can save two-thirds of the fare to most Asian destinations - if
you know which travel agents to buy your tickets through."

"What can you do to survive such notoriously unpleasant business
centres as Bogota, Lagos and Frankfurt?"

"How can you obtain an (almost palatable) meal in Moscow in under
two hours?"

"How can you check you are not paying too much for your air travel?"

The answers to these and other travel questions can be found in BUSINESS
TRAVELLER. Launched in the autumn of 1976 in London, and now published ten times
a year, BUSINESS TRAVELLER provides frequent travellers with a single, reliable and
independent source of information on how to get the best value for money when travelling.

BUSINESS TRAVELLER could save you or your company thousands
of pounds in air fares

On some routes across the Atlantic, to and from the Far East, and within the USA
and Europe, air fares can vary by as much as 400%. But, uncovering these fares can
be a complex and time-consuming task in which your travel agent is often unable or
unwilling to help. In every issue of BUSINESS TRAVELLER you will find an Instant-
Reference Fares Guide which tells you what air travel savings are available on flights
to Asia, Africa, North and South America, and within Europe, where to obtain the
tickets, and exactly which fare to ask for.

The following examples show fares based on confirmed seats with no restrictions:

Destination	Standard economy return fare	Alternative fare in Business Traveller	You save
London - Frankfurt	£ 155	£ 55	£ 100
London - Rome	£ 289	£ 95	£ 194
London - Cairo	£ 512	£ 225	£ 287
Frankfurt - Dubai	DM 3914	DM 1738	DM 2176
Dhahran - London	£ 305	£ 153	£ 152
Amsterdam - Tokyo	Dfl 6739	Dfl 2500	Dfl 4239
Bahrain - Los Angeles (via Bangkok)	£ 700	£ 376	£ 324
Singapore - Sydney	S$ 3138	S$ 1200	S$ 1938
London - Rio de Janeiro	£1274	£ 600	£ 674

Export Times Publishing Ltd., Registered Office: 60/61 Fleet St., London EC4Y 1LA. Registered in England no: 1137442. Cables: Exportimes London EC4. VAT no: 244 899317

A Look at these sections before you read the text:

1 VOCABULARY

destination the place you are going to
notoriously famous in a negative way
palatable with a good taste
launched started
reliable you can trust and believe it
(to) vary (to) be different; (to) change
task job
restrictions things you cannot do

Now read the text and answer the skim questions.

2 SKIM

a Who is this letter from? What is it selling?
b What are you expected to do after reading the letter?

B Look at these sections after reading the text:

3 COMPREHENSION

a What service does *Business Traveller* offer?
b When did the magazine start?
c How can you save money on tickets to Asian destinations?
d How much can you save on a flight from London to Rio?

4 INFERENCE

a Why isn't the price of the magazine given?
b What is implied by 'your travel agent is often . . . unwilling to help'?
c What is implied about life or business in Moscow? Why are there brackets (. . .) around the phrase 'almost palatable'?

5 REFERENCE

a What is 'economy class'?
b Look at the address of *Business Traveller*. What is this address usually associated with?
c What currency is S$?

6 LANGUAGE

Every business has its own jargon. In the travel business, words like *economy class* are used for simple ideas like 'normal price'. Try to explain the simple meaning of these other words of travel business jargon:

a stopover
b round trip
c club class
d OK status
e bucket shop
f jet lag
g APEX

7 OPINION

a Why do you think it is possible to have different prices for the same flight? What is the cause of this?
b How can the magazine get information about cheap fares that is not available to the normal businessperson?
c Are all these cheap tickets legal? If so, is it right that some people should pay less than others? Should the airlines or the government stop this?
d If it is true that travel agents are unable or unwilling to help, why would this be?

8 WRITING

a Write to *Business Traveller*, asking about the subscription price.
b Imagine you want to fly from London to Rio. Your travel agent gives you the price listed in the table, £1,274. Write out the conversation you would have with the travel agent, explaining that you think you can get a ticket for £600.

Test your ability as a decision-maker.

So you think you're a good decision-maker? Here's your chance to prove it. Below are a number of simple business-related problems you could face during the course of a month. Let's see how well you do. Answers at the bottom of the page.

1 You are about to set off on a long business trip. You'd planned to take the car but the forecast is 'fog'. Do you:
(a) catch a train instead?
(b) think 'Oh hell' and take the car anyway?
(c) ring in sick?

2 You're travelling to meet the client for a 'working lunch' to celebrate the new contract. Do you:
(a) assume 'working' means 'wining' and leave the car behind?
(b) trust that – touch wood – you've often driven after a few drinks without ever being involved in an accident?
(c) resent the mere suggestion that you might be more comfortable (not to mention safer) going by train?

3 The Chairman asks you to represent the company at an all day conference in Devon. Do you:
(a) book an Inter-City Sleeper for the journey down; travel home by Inter-City 125?
(b) reluctantly decide on a pre-dawn drive down, returning home at midnight?
(c) get your secretary to find out about the nightlife in Plymouth?

4 Your company car goes in for its annual service. Do you:
(a) look forward to a period of civilised business travel by train?
(b) insist on an equally prestigious car from the car pool?
(c) sulk when the replacement turns out to be 7 years old?

5 Tomorrow you are to travel to an important business prospect. It's crucial you make a good impression but pressure of work means you're less prepared than you'd like to be. Do you:
(a) take the train so you can catch up on your homework?
(b) hope you'll be able to talk around any awkward points?
(c) cancel the meeting?

6 When you get home from a business trip do you:
(a) kiss your wife?
(b) scowl at your wife?
(c) kick the cat?

Answers

If you answered (a) in each case you're an excellent decision-maker–prospects very good. If you answered (a) in only some of the cases you could improve your effectiveness by making greater use of the train. If you answered (a) in none of the cases, write 'This is the age of the train' 1000 times.

This is the age of the train ⇒

A Look at these sections before you read the text:

1 VOCABULARY

during the course of within (a period of time)
forecast weather news for today
(to) ring in sick (to) telephone to explain you are ill
touch wood if you are lucky; (touching wood, literally, is said to bring luck)
wining entertaining clients with drinks
(to) resent (to) feel angry about something
reluctantly unhappily; you don't want to do it
prestigious high-class
(to) sulk (to) look unhappy when you are angry; (to) not speak

2 SKIM

a What is this quiz really testing?
b What are you expected to do after reading this advertisement?

Now read the text and answer the skim questions.

B Look at these sections after reading the text:

3 COMPREHENSION

a What do all these 'problems' have in common?
b Why is the company car not available? (question 4)
c Why are you less prepared than you should be? (question 5)
d What is the reason for travelling to Devon? (question 3)

4 INFERENCE

a How can you tell that the advertisement is encouraging the use of trains rather than cars? Is it very obvious?
b What is the suggestion behind 'working means wining', when talking about the working lunch? (question 2)
c Why should anyone want to kick the cat? (question 6)

5 REFERENCE

a What is Devon? Where is it?
b What is an Inter-City Sleeper? What is the Inter-City 125?
c What is a car pool?
d What and where is Plymouth?

6 LANGUAGE

Look at this sentence from the text:
   *You are about to **set off** on a long business trip.*
To set off is a phrasal verb—a verb with *on, off, in, up,* for example. Find the phrasal verbs in the advertisement which have these meanings:
a to be taken to a garage for repair
b to find time to do work you haven't yet done
c to depart on a journey
d to be happy about something happening in the future
e to prove to be (unexpectedly); to have the result that

7 OPINION

a Do the quiz yourself, and write down your decisions. Then turn the page around and look at the answers.
b Do you agree with the descriptions given in the answers? What do you think of the test? Is it a good advertisement for trains?
c What do you think is meant by the advertisement's phrase, 'This is the age of the train'?
d Do you agree with the idea that the train is a better form of business transport than the car? Why?/Why not?

8 WRITING

a Write a memo to senior management explaining how trains could be more effective on business trips than cars. Explain how the company could save money this way.
b Write the text for an advertisement by a car manufacturer, showing that it is cheaper and better to travel by car on a business trip. You can refer to this train advertisement.

New international economic "think-tank"

A new private, nonprofit economic research institute which will be concerned exclusively with policy issues in international economic affairs, the Institute for International Economics (IIE), is being set up in Washington, D.C., funded by a $4 million grant from the German Marshall Fund of the United States. C. Fred Bergsten, a well-known U.S. international economist who was Assistant U.S. Secretary of the Treasury for International Affairs, 1977-81, will be director of the institute. Dr. Bergsten also has served on the senior staff of the National Security Council, 1969-71, and as a senior fellow of the Brookings Institution, another prominent Washington "think-tank."

Frank E. Loy, president of the German Marshall Fund of the United States, said the purpose of the new institute is to strengthen the formulation of international economic policy, particularly in the United States, and to lift the level of public debate in that critical area. The policy area is especially important to maintaining a healthy relationship among the industrialized countries, which will be the primary focus of research, he added.

Research will be undertaken into a wide range of international economic issues, including trade, international monetary affairs, investment, energy, commodities, and North-South and East-West economic relations. The studies will focus on the medium-term horizon (a one- to three-year period), which is deemed especially crucial to policy formulation. Results of the studies will be communicated primarily through a series of Papers on International Economics and through briefings and seminars, both in Washington and elsewhere.

Additionally, the institute hopes to help communicate research findings in the field of international economics, from whatever source throughout the world, more effectively to those concerned with policy both in and outside governments.

The institute will be governed by a board of directors chaired by Peter G. Peterson, former U.S. Secretary of Commerce who is currently chairman of the New York-based investment group, Lehman Brothers Kuhn Loeb. Richard N. Cooper, former U.S. Under Secretary of State for Economic Affairs and currently professor of economics at Harvard University, will be chairman of an advisory committee which will be responsible for setting a precise agenda for research. The agenda will be chosen through an ongoing process of consultations with officials of governments and international organizations, the private sector, and observers of international economic affairs in academic and other research institutions.

From *Economic Impact*, issue 38, 1982, published by US Information Agency, Washington DC.

A Look at these sections before you read the text:

1 VOCABULARY

think-tank group of experts who study certain problems
funded by paid for by
senior fellow professor or senior teacher in a university
prominent important
deemed considered; judged
crucial very important; central to the problem
briefing meeting to give information on a topic
ongoing continuing

Now read the text and answer the skim questions.

2 SKIM

a Who is organising this new think-tank? Where is it?
b What will be the purpose of this think-tank?

B Look at these sections after reading the text:

3 COMPREHENSION

a Who is paying for the new think-tank?
b Who will be the director of the institute?
c What will it study?
d How will its results be published?
e In what way will the studies be restricted?

4 INFERENCE

a Is this new think-tank independent of the government, or part of it? What evidence is there?
b Who will decide what the institute should study? What difference does it make?
c Why is the 'medium-term' considered crucial to economic policy?

5 REFERENCE

a What does D.C. stand for?
b What is the German Marshall Fund?
c What is the National Security Council?

6 LANGUAGE

Look at this sentence from the text:
  The policy area is especially important to maintaining
  . . .
This is another way of saying:
  The policy area is especially important to the maintenance of . . .
Change these sentences so that they use the *-ing* form:

a He is in charge of the distribution of office machinery.
b This department is concerned with the supervision of the accounts.
c We're very interested in the development of new products.
d The board is currently involved in the assessment of new proposals.
e Our salesmen are tired of the presentation of outdated products.

7 OPINION

a Why are think-tanks considered useful? Do you think they make helpful and practical suggestions?
b In what areas are think-tanks most likely to be useful and successful?
c Are think-tanks like the one in the text likely to be controlled by governments? How could a government persuade a think-tank to produce the right results?
d Would you work in a think-tank, if you were asked? Give your reasons.

8 WRITING

a Write a brief summary of the main facts of the text, for the Chief Economist in your Head Office. What do you think he or she will be most interested in?
b Write a letter to the Institute for International Economics, asking for details of their seminars and their publications. Suggest that you would like to speak at their seminars, or to write a paper for them.

New York City is open for businesses.

No other city in America offers more financial incentives to expand or re-locate your business.

Every new business we attract to New York City brings with it more jobs, more money, more everything for the economic vitality of the city.

That's why we're offering the most comprehensive package of financial incentives of any city in America. Incentives which can actually equal or exceed your capital investment.

Up to 100% tax exempt financing.

The New York City Industrial Development Agency is empowered to offer qualified businesses that expand or re-locate in New York City the availability of 100% tax-exempt financing. Plus substantial real estate tax abatements and other financial incentives.

Substantial savings available.

The IDA package, including low-interest, tax-exempt financing, real estate tax abatements, certain sales tax exemptions, and numerous other benefits can lead to savings of 50% to 125% of your capital investment.

The entire package can be wrapped and ready to go in 45 to 90 days.

Our people have one mission: to bring new businesses to New York City. They're informed, resourceful professionals who have the experience to help you achieve your objectives in as little time as possible.

The most fertile business climate in the world.

There are over 190,000 businesses in New York City. Nowhere will you find a larger concentration of national and international buyers, sellers, customers and prospects than New York City. Not to mention the largest financial community, the most extensive communications, shipping and service facilities, as well as a highly experienced and motivated labor force.

Can you really afford to overlook New York City?

It's your move.

Join the many companies that have moved to New York City. Find out if your business qualifies for assistance under the New York City Industrial Development Agency program. Send in the coupon below, or give us a call.

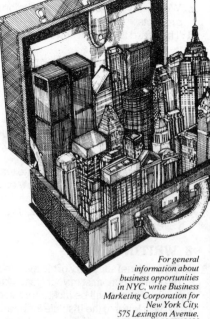

For general information about business opportunities in NYC, write Business Marketing Corporation for New York City, 575 Lexington Avenue, New York, N.Y. 10022

THE NYC IDA — **New York City Industrial Development Agency**
225 Broadway—Room 1200
New York, New York 10007
(212) 267-9600

AW-8-80

Sirs: Please send me your brochure on financial and real estate tax benefits in New York City.

Name _____

Company _____ Title _____

Type of business _____

Address _____

City _____ State/Country _____ Zip _____

New York City Industrial Development Agency, 225 Broadway, Room 1200, New York, N.Y. 10007, Harold Ross, Executive Director

A Look at these sections before you read the text:

1 VOCABULARY

vitality energy; life
incentives encouragements; *here*, money or loans to help businesses start in New York
empowered given the power by government
tax-exempt free from tax
abatements reductions
real estate property—land or buildings (USA only)
extensive wide, complete; including everything

Now read the text and answer the skim questions.

2 SKIM

a What is the advertisement trying to achieve?
b What is the job of the agency who placed the advertisement?

B Look at these sections after reading the text:

3 COMPREHENSION

a How many businesses are there in New York?
b How quickly is it possible to get these business incentives?
c What are the incentives offered? Give four incentives to move your business to New York.
d What are the other advantages of having your business in New York?

4 INFERENCE

a Why does the city offer these financial incentives? How can they afford to spend the city's money like this?
b What could the 'numerous other benefits' be? What would you expect?
c Why is the service so quick—financing in only 45 days?

5 REFERENCE

a What could a 'qualified' business refer to?
b What is sales tax?

6 LANGUAGE

Some American words or phrases are slightly different from those of British English. There are several examples in this text. Try to find the American words or phrases for these British English meanings:
a postcode
b write to . . .
c workforce
d VAT
e property
f complete and ready to be collected
g give us a ring

7 OPINION

a What do you think the illustration is trying to suggest?
b Do you think this package of incentives would make you want to move your business to New York?
c What, in your opinion, are the good and bad points of moving to New York, from both a business and personal point of view?
d Do you think it is cost-effective for the city to spend money on financing new businesses? Is this policy used in your city?

8 WRITING

a Write to the New York IDA, explaining your business and asking for further details.
b Imagine you run a small business and you have decided to move to New York. Write a memorandum to all your staff, explaining what is going to happen. Point out that they can move with you, or lose their jobs. Explain what sort of compensation they can expect.

The Economist
Intelligence Unit

SPENCER HOUSE, 27 ST. JAMES'S PLACE, LONDON SW1A 1NT

Telephone 01-493 6711 Telex 266353 Cables ECONUNIT LONDON SW1

P824

Dear Sir,

In order to make the most profitable decisions, it is essential to
have more, and better information on all the relevant issues. This
is especially true in todays extremely harsh economic climate.
Unfortunately, the sheer volume of source material has itself become
a major obstacle and there can be problems in securing data that is
both reliable and relevant.

The EIU's publications cut through the difficulty by bringing
together a concise information service on a wide range of important
subjects in a form precisely designed to meet the needs of managers
and administrators.

The Quarterly Economic Reviews, for example, provide regular and
comprehensive analysis of economic developments in all commercially
significant countries. A series of regional Quarterly Energy
Reviews offer a similar service on energy trends.

Other regular services cover consumer markets in the UK and
Western Europe, the international automotive, rubber, paper and
packaging and tourism industries, as well as developments in multi-
national corporate enterprise, European integration and trends in
the UK economy.

Backing up the regular publications are individual research-based
Special Reports each giving in-depth treatment to a topic of major
interest. Even more specialised and detailed market research
reports are provided by EIU Multi-Client Studies which usually deal
with product group sub-sectors, often in a number of different
countries.

We believe that in the enclosed leaflets describing our publications
and reports you will find something which will meet your own
particular information needs; an order form and reply envelope are
enclosed.

Yours faithfully,

W. Bull
Business Director

Enc

The Economist Intelligence Unit Limited : Registered Office as above : Registered in England No. 563972

A Look at these sections before you read the text:

1 VOCABULARY

harsh very difficult
climate state; situation
sheer volume the amount of information itself is a problem
concise summarised; in a short form
comprehensive including everything
corporate involving large companies
in-depth with great detail

Now read the text and answer the skim questions.

2 SKIM

a What service does the EIU provide?
b What has been enclosed with the letter?

B Look at these sections after reading the text:

3 COMPREHENSION

a What do businesspeople need in order to make a profit?
b What is the problem that EIU can solve?
c What are the Quarterly Energy Reviews?
d What markets does EIU cover?

INFERENCE

a EIU is not the only company to sell information on business. What do they suggest is better about their service?
b What sort of problems can there be in securing data? What is the implication of this?

5 REFERENCE

a What is the connection between the EIU and the *Economist* magazine? Could they be the same company? Suggest why.
b What do you think European integration refers to?

6 LANGUAGE

Look at these words from the text:
  harsh   economic   climate
The word *harsh* is a little formal or exaggerated for normal spoken English. In conversation we would probably say *difficult* or *hard*. Try and find the words in the text which are formal or exaggerated, which have the same meaning as these words:

a difficulty
b getting
c exactly
d car
e companies
f great

7 OPINION

a Can you find the punctuation mistake in the letter? Do you think it's an important one?
b Do you think this service is too specialised for big companies? Could it be useful for the ordinary businessperson?
c Do you think that selling information in this way could be a profitable business for the *Economist*? Is it possible to sell the same information to different companies? Is it right?

8 WRITING

a Write to the EIU explaining what your business area is. Ask them if they have any special reports on your area.
b Imagine you are writing a letter like this to sell your company's services. How would you organise the letter? Write a draft.

It contains 462 rules.
If any advertiser breaks one, we throw the book at him.

The British Code of Advertising Practice is a set of rules to which any advertiser must adhere when he places advertisements in a newspaper, magazine, on a poster, in a cinema, or in direct mail.

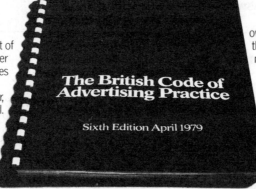

Every year, millions of advertisements appear. All but a small number comply with the Code and are legal, decent, honest and truthful.

It's the job of the Advertising Standards Authority, in the consumer's interest, to weed out those offenders and, as our name suggests, to keep advertising up to standard.

That means that no advertisement can continue to run if it in any way contravenes the British Code of Advertising Practice. And that applies to the spirit of the Code, as well as to the letter.

To give you an idea of the sort of rules the Code contains, here is an example:

II. 3. Advertisements should not be so framed as to abuse the trust of consumers or exploit their lack of experience or knowledge.

Who sits on the Council of the ASA?

The Advertising Standards Authority is an independent body.

Although it is financed by the advertising industry (who are incidentally as interested as is the consumer in banning unacceptable advertising), it works independently of the industry.

It has to be independent to be fair and unbiased about complaints.

For this reason, the Chairman is independent and so are the majority of the Council members.

For instance, in the last year we have had a Methodist Minister, a consumerist and a Member of the House of Lords on the Council.

Under the Council's supervision, a full-time secretariat works to make sure that the Code is being adhered to by the advertising industry. And that decisions made by the Advertising Standards Authority are being enforced.

What happens to an advertiser who breaks the Code?

If we believe the consumer's complaint is valid, we contact the advertiser. He will be instructed to remove the advertisement or amend it accordingly.

Because advertisers know we have teeth, the system works very quickly and effectively.

It also has the blessing of the

owners of the vast majority of the country's newspapers, magazines, poster sites and cinemas, who don't hesitate to withdraw an advertisement which contravenes the Code and who would not run an advertisement which we have banned. (By the way, TV and radio advertising are dealt with by the I.B.A.)

Does the ASA keep up with changing attitudes in society?

We carry out consumer research into areas of interest. For instance, at the moment, we are looking into children's reactions to advertising. Having assessed the research findings, we will amend the Code if we feel it is out-of-date.

Does the ASA simply react to complaints from the public?

No. We conduct our own monitoring system. We regularly look at specific areas of advertising and check that advertisers are adhering to the Code without being prompted to do so.

So, if any advertiser does offend the Code, he knows what will happen to him. He'll get the book thrown at him. And it will hit where it hurts him most; at his business.

If you'd like to know more about the way we operate, please write to us at the address below. ✓

The Advertising Standards Authority.
If an advertisement is wrong, we're here to put it right.
ASA Ltd., Brook House, Torrington Place, London WC1E 7HN.

A Look at these sections before you read the text:

1 VOCABULARY

(to) throw the book at (to) punish someone for a lot of reasons
code collection of rules
(to) comply with (to) follow the rules
(to) weed out (to) find and get rid of something
(to) contravene (to) break the rules
framed written; planned
(to) amend (to) make better
blessing approval

Now read the text and answer the skim questions.

2 SKIM

a Who pays for the Advertising Standards Authority (ASA)?
b What sort of advertising does it study?

B Look at these sections after reading the text:

3 COMPREHENSION

a What does the ASA do with advertisements?
b How does it find out that some advertisements are bad?
c What does the ASA tell the avertiser to do?
d What sort of research does the ASA carry out?

4 INFERENCE

a Why is such an organisation paid for by the people it is checking? What is the advantage for the advertising industry?
b Why should the advertising industry be 'as interested as is the consumer in banning unacceptable advertising'?

5 REFERENCE

a What is a Methodist Minister?
b What is a Member of the House of Lords? What does he/she do?
c What does the IBA refer to? If it deals with radio and TV, what must the B mean?

6 LANGUAGE

Look at this sentence from the text:
> **Having assessed** the research findings, we will amend the Code.

This means the same as:
> **After we have assessed** the research findings, we will amend the Code.

and it is used to join two actions in a sequence.
Join these sentences together in the same way:
a we receive a complaint/we study the advertisement
b we study the advertisement/we decide if it is misleading
c we decide on its quality/we write to the advertiser
d we write to the advertiser/we wait for his reaction
e we decide to ban an advertisement/we inform all the newspapers

7 OPINION

a Do you think it is necessary to check the quality and content of advertising? What are the advantages and disadvantages of such controls?
b What would happen to advertising if there were no controls on it? Could anything dangerous happen?
c If the ASA is paid for by the advertising industry, would you agree that it can still be independent?
d How is advertising controlled in your country? Should it be more or less controlled than it is now? Why?/Why not?

8 WRITING

a Write a short letter to the ASA asking for details of the rules affecting the advertising of your products or services. Explain what you want to put in your advertising.
b Write a memo to your advertising manager, asking if he or she knows about advertising controls in different countries. Ask the advertising manager to explain them to you.

Carpetbagger

PHIL HARRIS, the retailer who turned an inheritance of three shops into an empire of 380.

PHIL HARRIS was hurtled into the business world at an age when most of today's teenagers are battling with "O" levels. His father was under 40 when he died, leaving Phil, still only 15, to run three South London carpet shops. He faced a daunting choice—to sell out or run the shops himself. He decided to have a go.

Now, less than 25 years later, Phil Harris is one of the most successful men in retailing. His stake in Harris Queensway is worth £20m. When he took over the original three shops, sales were running at £75,000 a year. This year, Harris Queensway with 380 outlets will turn over around £170m.

At the start Harris' sole ambition was to keep the business afloat. He soon adopted a policy of "expand and keep on going." This is still his motto. Doing business has got easier. When he began he needed to get a guarantor whenever he signed a deal, as he was under 21.

The first shop he bought was in South London's Balham High Street. The leasehold cost £12,500. It is still one of the group's outlets. Success did not come automatically. By 1960, still under 20, he had expanded the business but with limited success.

The turning point came with a 3,000 sq ft store in East Ham. This was a very big carpet store for those days. It was a bit of a gamble but one that turned up trumps.

In 1972 Harris clinched what he describes as his best ever deal. He bought the Keith Rayle chain from Combined

English Stores for £750,000. The biggest acquisition was still to come.

Five years later Harris paid £2m for Queensway, a discount warehouse operation. Going public in 1978 was another milestone. He pocketed £6.5m from selling part of his stake.

Harris has accumulated the usual trappings of wealth. He says modestly he lives "quite well." This means a more-than-pleasant home in Kent with a swimming pool and a Mercedes in the drive. Being a millionaire has allowed him to indulge his hobbies. He has a string of showjumpers led by "Mr Ross" with David Broome in the saddle.

His main relaxation is sport. In the mid-1950s he qualified for the Wimbledon juniors. He admits to being too old for football now but still plays the odd game of tennis or cricket.

Not surprisingly for a multi-millionaire he is a workaholic. He says he dislikes holidays and when he takes them, is always ringing up the office to check what is going on.

Terry Garrett

From the *Financial Times*, 24 December 1981. Reproduced with permission.

A Look at these sections before you read the text:

1 VOCABULARY

hurtled rushed; thrown (into the business)
daunting challenging; frightening
(to) have a go (to) try and succeed
stake share
outlets shops or selling points
afloat not sinking; *here*, (to) keep business alive
turned up trumps was successful
clinched (a deal) completed; made a deal
trappings external signs

2 SKIM

a What is Phil Harris's business?
b When did he become a millionaire?

Now read the text and answer the skim questions.

B Look at these sections after reading the text:

3 COMPREHENSION

a How did Phil Harris get control of his business?
b What was his philosophy for making money?
c What was his problem until he was 21?
d What does he think was his best deal?
e What does he do in his free time?

4 INFERENCE

a What are the implied reasons for his success in business?
b What was the gamble involved in the East Ham store?
c Why was the Keith Rayle deal the 'best ever'?
d Why does Harris talk about living only 'quite well', when he is a millionaire with a swimming pool, a big house and so on?

5 REFERENCE

a What are 'O' levels? Why do people 'battle' with them?
b What is a discount warehouse? What business does it do?
c What does 'going public' involve, and what are the benefits?
d What does 'Wimbledon juniors' refer to?

6 LANGUAGE

Look at this sentence from the text:
> He says he dislikes holidays. . . and **is always ringing up** the office to check what is going on.

The use of the continuous tense indicates that the action is strange or negative in some way, for example:
> He's always complaining

indicates that he continually complains, and the speaker does not like this.
Rewrite these sentences using *is always + -ing.*
a My boss continually criticises my work.
b My children continually play their pop records too loud.
c My wife continually asks me to repaint the living room.
d My relatives continually ask me to lend them money.

7 OPINION

a If you were Phil Harris, what decision would you have made at the age of 15? Would you have taken control of the business?
b Why was it necessary for Harris to get a guarantor for his deals when he was under 21? Is this unfair on young businesspeople?
c What makes Phil Harris and others like him a 'workaholic'? Why does he find it difficult to take a holiday? Do you feel the same?
d Phil Harris has a Mercedes, a big house and a swimming pool, and he owns show horses. Do you think this is the reason he works so hard? Can he enjoy these 'trappings of success' if he works so hard?

8 WRITING

a Imagine you are Phil Harris. Write a description of how it feels to be a millionaire before the age of 40.
b Imagine you are organising a management training course. You would like Phil Harris to speak at the conference about the management secret behind successful and profitable business. Write him a letter asking if he will come.
c How would you plan to become a millionaire? Write about your plan.

DAVID HUTCHINS ASSOCIATES
Industrial Training Specialists

IF JAPAN CAN...
SO CAN WE

A two day Conference demonstrating dramatically
the achievements of some British companies who are
meeting the Japanese challenge – and winning!

Programme

DAY 1

9.00–9.30
Registration and Coffee.

9.30–10.00
Opening address by Dr W. R. Thoday, President
European Organisation for Quality Control.

10.00
Company wide Quality Control – David Hutchins.

Invented in the West, manufactured in Japan –
exported back to the West!

A study of Modern Japanese Management
philosophy, its development and comparison with
the Western situation. The paper is intended to
stimulate a complete re-think by Western companies
to the role of quality in an organisation and their
ability to survive in an increasingly competitive
world. The paper disputes the whole basis of quality
control as understood by Western organisations
and offers the establishment of a fundamentally
different role for this vital aspect of market success
and price competitiveness.

12.30–2.00
Drinks and Luncheon.

2.00–4.30
A structure for implementation in Western organisations. Time scale, corporate planning, the roles of
senior management, middle management, the
specialists and organised labour. The importance
of training, and expected results. The first five years
in outline.

4.30–5.00
Discussion and brainstorming of questions to be
answered on Day 2.

DAY 2

9.30–10.30
Discussion of questions arising from Day 1.

10.30
**PRESENTATIONS FROM SUCCESSFUL
COMPANIES**

1. WEDGWOOD LTD. This World famous company
committed themselves totally to the implementation
of Company wide Quality Control just over one year
ago and already have over 78 Quality Circles in
training and operation. The Wedgwood programme
is probably the best developed in Western Europe.

In this Session, a Quality Circle will demonstrate
their achievements since formation.

2. MULLARD LTD, SOUTHAMPTON. Mullard began
the development of Quality Circles after an extensive
quality awareness programme. Circles have sub-
sequently grown at the rate of 5 new Circles every
three months at the Southampton factory. This
presentation will show how Circles can operate in
the demanding field of high quality electronics.

3. ABBEY HOSIERY MILLS LTD. One of the many
companies in the clothing industry to have incorporated this concept. Abbey are unique in having
arranged for a presentation to have been given to

the entire Workforce at the local Civic Centre prior to
implementation. Enthusiasm for Quality Circles is
enormous at Abbey and this is evident in the work of
their newly formed groups.

4. CUMBRIA ENGINEERING were one of the first
heavy engineering companies to introduce Quality
Circles in Western Europe, and the first in British
Steel.

5. JOHN COLLIER MENSWEAR. Although new to
Quality Circles, two other Circles from this company
have already had their names in lights. One Circle
recently gave a public presentation at a seminar
organised by the Clothing and Footwear Institute.

4.30–4.45
Final summary by Dr Thoday and David Hutchins.
Closure.

D.H.A – PACESETTERS IN INDUSTRIAL TRAINING
Interest in Japan and its approach to industrial
management has grown to such an extent that the
subject has become a bandwagon for all sorts of
people. To see our pedigree in this work, just look at
our record . . .

1970   Examination paper set by David Hutchins
        required students to compare Quality Circles
        with "Zero Defects" an idea popular at that
        time.

1971   onwards – Quality Circles and the Concept of
        Total Quality Control featured in all Manage-
        ment of Quality Assurance Short Courses
        organised by David Hutchins at Slough
        College of Higher Education and occasional
        lectures at Ashridge Management College.

1977   David Hutchins organised the first U.K.
        Conference which linked the importance of
        Quality Assurance to Changing Liability
        Legislation and subsequently co-authored a
        book on the topic, published by Heineman.
        – Organised three day Conference coining
        the term "Product Risk Appraisal". Sub-
        sequently companies have been formed by
        others specifically to further this approach.

1978   Trained first company in Quality Circles.
        Organised first major Conference entitled
        "Quality Assurance aspects of Micro Elec-
        tronics". Subsequently hundreds of others
        have been organised by other organisations.

1979   "Japanese Approach to Product Quality
        Management" Conference sparked the U.K.
        and European interest in Quality Circles.
        David Hutchins Associates formed.

1980   Visit by Japanese Quality Circle team – 22
        Japanese Managers and Foremen gave
        presentations at Conference organised by
        David Hutchins at the Waldorf, London.
        "World Convention on Quality Circles"
        held at the Waldorf with speakers from
        Australia, Brazil, Germany, Japan, Norway,
        Sweden, U.K. and U.S.A.

Since 1978, we have trained over 55 companies in
Quality Circles and some of these now have the best
developed Quality Circle programmes in Europe.

© **David Hutchins Associates.**

A Look at these sections before you read the text:

1 VOCABULARY

re-think new ideas on a well-known subject
disputes disagrees with
vital very important
luncheon formal word for 'lunch'
time-scale the plan of what happens over a period of time
brainstorming finding answers to problems by open discussion
implementation the carrying out, putting into practice, of a plan
pedigree history; record of the past

Now read the text and answer the skim questions.

2 SKIM

a What connection has this seminar with Japan? Why is Japan mentioned?
b Which company will demonstrate its quality circle work here?

B Look at these sections after reading the text:

3 COMPREHENSION

a How long is the seminar?
b What does the seminar discuss?
c Why is the Wedgwood company making a presentation?
d When did David Hutchins start to talk about quality circles?
e What was Hutchins' book about?

4 INFERENCE

a What is the aim of the seminar? Is it clear?
b What is a quality circle? Is this explained in the programme? Why not?
c Is David Hutchins a businessman or a teacher? What information can you find that suggests what he does?
d Why are quality circles and Japanese management so interesting to British managers?

5 REFERENCE

a What is the European Organisation for Quality Control?
b What is the Wedgwood company famous for?
c What is British Steel?
d What is Slough College of Higher Education? What is the connection with quality circles?

6 LANGUAGE

Look at this sentence from the text:
 One of the many companies **to have incorporated** this concept. . .
This is one way of giving extra information. You could also use *which* or *who*:
 One of the many companies *which have incorporated this concept*. . .
Now re-write these sentences using *to have* + past participle:
a This is one of the companies which have started quality circles.
b He is one of the first UK experts who have studied quality circles.
c This is our first product which has been re-designed by a quality circle.

7 OPINION

a Why do you think David Hutchins formed his company, DHA? What else do you think the company might do, as well as give seminars?
b What do you think of quality circles? Have you had any experience of them? If not, what methods does your company use to check the quality of its output?
c What do you think of the Japanese management philosophy? Are quality circles the most important part of the philosophy?
d Could you introduce quality circles into your company? How would workers and management react to such meetings?

8 WRITING

a Write a summary of the seminar programme, in a memo to your boss. Suggest that someone from the company goes to the seminar.
b Write a report on quality control in your company—how it works, how it could be improved and so on.

Management Course

Alan W. Pearson, B.Sc.
*Senior Lecturer in Decision Analysis; Director of the Management
Course; Director, R & D Research Unit*

After some years' industrial experience, Alan Pearson became Lecturer
in Economic Statistics at Manchester University and has been Director of
the R & D Research Unit at MBS since 1967. He is an active participant
on a wide range of management and educational committees, a member
of the editorial board of **IEEE Transactions on Engineering Management**
and Editor of **R & D Management.** He has published widely in scientific
and management journals and is co-author of **Mathematics for Economists**
(David & Charles, 1975).

Course Participants and Selection Criteria

The 10-week residential executive development
programme is intended for men and women
who have already demonstrated a high degree
of competence in their organisation and who
are seen as likely to undertake wider
responsibilities in the near future.

Selection is normally based on information
contained in the application forms. However,
the School has found that the motivation of
course members is enhanced when they have
been closely associated with the decision to
send them to Manchester. For the same
reason, we strongly believe that both
participants and their nominating
organisations should have a clear view of the
level and type of responsibility they will be
expected to undertake on their return to work.

Objectives and Strategy

The aim of the course is to give members the
opportunity of further developing themselves
as effective managers.

The total resources of the School are made
available in a highly flexible way and each
course member is helped to construct and
follow a personal curriculum tailored to his
individual needs and those of his organisation.

Course Design The course is in three phases:—

Diagnosis

Phase One — the first three weeks of the course —
consists of plenary sessions (learning the
languages of the basic disciplines); educational
projects and business games. These are designed
to broaden course members' understanding of
complex organisations.

During this phase comes the "options
supermarket", when teaching staff briefly present
the content of the options and projects which
they will be offering later in the course.

The course member is then able to devise a
personal learning strategy by selecting the most
relevant of these options and projects.

Differentiation

Phase Two — the major part of the course —
lasts for about six weeks.

As in Phase One (but now less frequently),
plenary sessions continue to be devoted to the
major disciplines: micro- and macro-economics;
financial analysis; management information and
control systems; marketing; managerial
psychology; industrial relations; and theories of
organisational behaviour and organisation design.

Other types of learning situations are created and
developed in this phase
— individual projects of guided study
— seminars based on current research by
  members of staff
— field projects based on real-life situations
— small groups pursuing a topic from an earlier
  plenary session in greater depth
Several of the projects are especially designed to
relate individual subject disciplines to each other.

This is a brochure for a management course offered by the Manchester Business School.

A Look at these sections before you read the text:

1 VOCABULARY

residential where students live at the college
(to) undertake (to) accept; (to) take on
(in) the near future soon
enhanced increased; improved
plenary session when all members of a course are together
(to) devise (to) work out; (to) design; (to) organise

Now read the text and answer the skim questions.

2 SKIM

a How long is this management course?
b What is the aim of the course?

B Look at these sections after reading the text:

3 COMPREHENSION

a How are people selected for the course?
b What happens in Phase One of the course?
c What is the aim of using business games?
d In what way is Phase Two different?

4 INFERENCE

a Phase Three is not described here. How long is it?
b What is an 'options supermarket'?
c Why does the school say that course members 'should have a clear view of the level and type of responsibility' they will have later?

5 REFERENCE

a Find out what these abbreviations mean:
  B.Sc.   R & D   MBS   IEEE
b Who are 'David & Charles'?

6 LANGUAGE

Look at this sentence from the text:
  *. . . the projects which they **will be offering** later in the course.*
This sentence emphasises a particular time in the future, the day when they can say, 'We are offering these projects . . .'. Rewrite these sentences using the same form:
a The course will start on 1 December.
b Course participants will stay in a first-class hotel during the course.
c In Phase Two they will study financial analysis.
d At the end of Phase Two they will complete their own projects.

7 OPINION

a Do you think you can learn how to be an 'effective manager' in 10 weeks? How much could you learn on a 10-week course?
b What sort of options and projects would you expect to find on the course? What sort of project would you find most useful?
c Do you think it is a good idea that course members choose their own options and projects? Is this the best way to learn?

8 WRITING

a Write a letter to the business school asking for a place on their next 10-week course. Explain why you should be accepted, and what you want to learn from the course.
b Write a summary of the aims and content of the course, in a memo to your Personnel Manager. Advise him or her on which people to send on the course.

To Our Stockholders

For the seventh consecutive year Sperry has increased its revenue and earnings. That result could only have been achieved through careful planning and energetic execution by dedicated Sperry people throughout the world.

Now we are on the threshold of a new period that can provide even more opportunities for Sperry. You may wonder why we believe that, in the face of continued pessimism in the news, intensified competition, extreme inflation, mounting operating costs, international financial instability and many other pressures on our worldwide business.

The major reason is that Sperry products help businesses reduce costs, increase productivity and improve performance. The computer, for example, stands almost alone in the industrial marketplace as a product which has had a decreasing real cost over the years. The price of information has decreased by a factor of 1,000 since we introduced the first commercial computer 28 years ago.

While not all our businesses have that kind of performance to point to, all are extremely good inflation fighters, and we want to take some time in this letter to tell you about them and to discuss our progress and assess our prospects.

Here are the summary figures for fiscal year 1979. Details appear elsewhere in the report.

Revenue: Revenue was $4.18 billion, up 14.5% over fiscal year 1978. Revenue from customers outside the United States was $1.78 billion, 43% of the total.

Earnings: Net income rose 26.9% to $224.1 million, equal to primary earnings per share of $6.35.

Backlog: At March 31, 1979 backlog was $2.8 billion, up 18% over 1978.

Stockholders' Equity: Stockholders' equity increased to $1.63 billion, up 13.7% over last year.

Dividends: Dividends declared in fiscal year 1979 were $1.32 per share, 17.9% over last year.

These are good results and with the perspective of the past seven years it is appropriate to pause and take stock—to re-examine our progress and assess our prospects.

Emphasis on Fundamentals

Two principal factors will determine whether Sperry will continue its recent pattern of uninterrupted growth in revenue and earnings.

The first is the external environment, which is beyond the control of any management. It includes the action or inaction of governments, currency fluctuations, inflation, the level of interest rates and even the weather, for we are in the farm equipment business.

The second is the environment inside Sperry, and by that we mean how we manage our business in view of the external factors. One key to our past success has been an unchanging emphasis on the fundamentals of our business. For Sperry these factors are people, planning, communications, capital appropriations, and research and development.

People

As in any successful business enterprise, it is people who really determine Sperry's margins of success. We know, too, that certain important personal factors determine the interest of the individuals to help Sperry excel. Of course, all of us want to know we are being fairly compensated for our contribution to the company. Management works very hard to see that Sperry people receive wages and benefits that fairly recognize individual effort. Further, management constantly monitors such things as the quality of working conditions and equal opportunity for employment, training and career advancement. We endeavor to assure that our fellow employees are given encouragement and the means to suggest ways for Sperry to become a better company in terms of the products we make, services to our customers, internal communications and in other ways. Management is continually seeking ways to be more responsive to the people of Sperry, just as all of us are working as a team to meet the expectations of our customers and stockholders.

A Look at these sections before you read the text:

1 VOCABULARY

consecutive one following the other
execution carrying out of a plan
threshold doorway; *here*, beginning of a new period
mounting increasing
by a factor of 1,000 it has been divided by 1,000
(to) take stock (to) assess the situation
fluctuations changes above or below a certain level
external factors outside influences or situations

2 SKIM

a What are the main products sold by Sperry?
b Is the company doing better or worse than the year before?

Now read the text and answer the skim questions.

B Look at these sections after reading the text:

3 COMPREHENSION

a What were the earnings per share for the year described in the report?
b What is special about the computer business?
c How much did stockholders earn from Sperry in this year?
d What are the factors that Sperry cannot control in its business?
e What makes a business successful, according to Sperry?

4 INFERENCE

a Does the company feel good or bad about the results shown here?
b Why does the company feel that people are so important?
c What sort of 'important personal factors' make people more or less interested in helping the company?
d What effect could the action or inaction of governments have on Sperry's business?

5 LANGUAGE

Look at these words from the text:
*stockholder   fiscal   backlog   billion
endeavor*
Each of these is an example of American usage. In British English there is either a different word or a different spelling, or the same word has a different meaning. Find out and explain the British English differences.

6 OPINION

a Why do you think the cost of computers has fallen in the last 10–20 years, when other products have increased in price?
b What do you understand by the ideas 'fairly compensated for our contribution to the company' and 'quality of working conditions'? Do they mean the same to everybody?
c In what ways can management be 'more responsive to the people' of the company? What would you suggest?

7 WRITING

a Imagine you are a financial journalist. Write an article describing Sperry's annual report.
b Write a draft text, like this one, to go with the annual report of your company.

UNIT 25   J T Chadwick

TECALEMIT–CHADWICK LTD

Doncaster Hall, Montgomery Terrace Road,
Sheffield   S6 3DE
Telephone: 0742 28702

Member of the Tecalemit U.K. Group of Companies

50 Milk Street,	Unit 3, Northfield Ind. Est.,
Digbeth,	Beresford Avenue,
Birmingham B5 5TP	Wembley, Middlesex HA0 1XN
Telephone: 021 643 9571	Telephone: 01 902 7365

For the attention of the
Accounts Controller

Your Ref.

Our Ref.   DTP/cp

Date

Dear Sirs,

In today's 'tight money' conditions, we have been adopting a
fairly flexible attitude towards minor delays in payment.

However, we are finding the amount of credit we are allowed
by our suppliers is limited, and this must be reflected in the
approach we make towards the amount of extra credit we can
allow our Customers.

As we are a Service Industry, and exist by our 'Ex-Stock'
Policy to meet our Customers' requirements, it is clear that
our stock is available for the benefit of all our Customers,
and wishing to treat all our Customers fairly, we cannot
continue to allow extended credit to the few that take it.

With immediate effect we are dispensing with our Polite
Reminder System. Our Terms of Business are the same as most
other Companies - payment being due by the end of the month
after the month in which the goods were delivered. Once an
account becomes more than one month overdue, supplies are
likely to be withheld, until the account is returned to Terms.

We are finding that the free finance in the form of extra credit
is affecting the quality of service we offer, and we see no
reason to restrain the service to many for the sake of a few,
when we can make better use of our resources for the benefit
of all our Customers.

Yours faithfully,
TECALEMIT CHADWICK LIMITED

D.T. PARRY
Managing Director

A company registered in England No. 442555   Registered Office: Montgomery Terrace Road, Sheffield S6 3DE
Directors: P. G. F. Seldon C.Eng.,M.I.Mech.E., (Chairman) J. M. Bennett B.Sc.,C.Eng.,F.I.Mech.E., D. T. Parry

Reproduced by permission of D T Parry, Managing Director, Tecalemit Chadwick Ltd.

A Look at these sections before you read the text:

1 VOCABULARY

controller manager
tight money difficult to get credit
minor not important; small
ex-stock goods are available immediately from stock
dispensing with getting rid of; finishing
reminder letter to make you remember
due necessary; expected
(to) restrain (to) restrict; (to) hold back

Now read the text and answer the skim questions.

2 SKIM

a What is the purpose of the letter?
b What action should be taken by the person reading the letter?

B Look at these sections after reading the text:

3 COMPREHENSION

a What are Chadwick's terms of business and payment?
b What are they changing in their system? When does this change begin?
c What will happen to customers who do not pay their bills?
d What is the reason for this change in policy?

4 INFERENCE

a What did Chadwick's suppliers say to Chadwick Ltd? Was this the real cause of the change in policy?
b In what way could the extra credit they give at the moment affect 'the quality of service' Chadwick offer?

5 REFERENCE

a What are the 'tight money' conditions referred to in the letter?
b What does the Polite Reminder System refer to?

6 LANGUAGE

Look at this sentence from the text:
   . . . supplies **are likely to be withheld** . . .
This use of the passive form makes the sentence more indirect, more impersonal and therefore not so aggressive as
   we will withhold your supplies.
Rewrite these sentences in the same less direct way:
a If you do not pay, we will cut off your electricity.
b If you do not pay, we will inform the banks and credit institutes.
c If we receive no money, we will take you to court.
d If the court agrees with us, it will declare you bankrupt.
e If you don't cooperate, the court will send you to jail.

7 OPINION

a Do you think the Terms of Business described here are normal in most companies?
b Is the credit allowed a little long? Why not allow credit up to only 30 days after delivery?
c What will be saved by not sending Polite Reminders?
d Is this letter a good way to get customers to pay? It is very polite and indirect—would it be better to be more aggressive?

8 WRITING

a Imagine your company has received this letter. Your account with Chadwick Ltd is two months overdue. Write to them explaining about your account.
b Write a similar letter, which your company can send to its bad customers.

METHODS OF SELLING ABROAD

Once you have researched the market and gauged the potential demand for your product you will then need some form of representation abroad to find buyers, negotiate prices, settle specifications, arrange deliveries, etc.

Direct representation

For a variety of reasons – for example after-sales service – you may decide on direct investment in manufacture or distribution. Provided that you have the necessary Bank of England approval to invest money abroad, you can often do this either as a joint venture with a local concern or by establishing a subsidiary company. There will also be local legal requirements to be satisfied e.g. the type of company allowed, limits on foreign participation, taxation, repatriation of income and capital. Your local branch of Barclays International can obtain this local information for you, assist in preparing your application and arrange introductions to reputable overseas lawyers.

Indirect representation

AGENTS: Through agents you can administer the sales of your goods in overseas countries. Agents may be firms which can organise every aspect of distribution over a defined area or they may be individuals who will seek out buyers and put them in touch with you. Great care is needed in appointing agents as they will probably be entirely responsible for the success of your business in their territories. You may consider it desirable to appoint a local agent to act on your behalf should any dispute arise over, for example, payment or delivery of the goods. The powers of your local agent will depend on what you authorise him to do. In some countries the relationship between principal and agent is subject to detailed legislation.

FOREIGN BUYING HOUSES IN THE UK: Certain large American, Canadian and Japanese retail stores have buying agencies in the United Kingdom through whom they buy the bulk of their British goods. These buying houses can provide you with a ready and simple means of selling your goods in their countries.

CONFIRMING HOUSES: A confirming house acts as a buying agent for an overseas importer. You deal direct with the confirming house which will usually pay you for the goods, and will often attend to the necessary documentation, although you will be responsible for shipping the goods to their final destination.

EXPORT MERCHANTS: Export merchants buy goods direct from you. The transaction is almost the same as selling in your home market. Thus you will not have problems of carrying out market research or finding buyers. But you will have no control over marketing and hence the subsequent success or otherwise of your product.

A Look at these sections before you read the text:

1 VOCABULARY

gauged assessed, examined, estimated
joint venture partnership
repatriation sending back to your own country
reputable known to have a good reputation
(to) administer (to) organise
territories countries or areas under their control
principal the main business partner; company working
with the agent
the bulk of most of

Now read the text and answer the skim questions.

2 SKIM

a Find out what a confirming house does.
b What services are offered here?

B Look at these sections after reading the text:

3 COMPREHENSION

a What must you do first if you want to sell products abroad?
b Why is it necessary to have representatives abroad?
c What is the difference between an agent that is a company and an agent that is an individual?
d What is the advantage of working with a buying house?
e What does an export merchant do? What is the advantage of working with this type of company?

4 INFERENCE

a Why is 'great care' necessary in appointing agents? What effects can they have upon your business?
b What sort of legislation do some countries have about the 'relationship between principal and agent'? What sort of restrictions could this involve?
c If you trade with an export merchant you will have no control over marketing. What effect could this have on sales? What sort of problems might occur?

5 REFERENCE

a What does 'Bank of England approval' refer to? What is necessary?
b Who are the 'certain large American, Canadian and Japanese retail stores' who have buying houses? Are they well known?

6 LANGUAGE

Look at this sentence from the text:
    . . . *should any dispute arise over payment or delivery of the goods.*
This is a more formal way of saying:
    . . . *if any dispute arises over payment . . .*
Notice that with *should* there is no '*s*' on the end of the verb *arise*. This is the subjunctive.

Now make *should. . .* sentences from these examples:
a If the machine breaks down, call this number.
b We will meet on Monday if the situation has got any worse.
c We have got extra stocks to bring in if demand increases.
d A local agent is very useful if any legal problem occurs.

7 OPINION

a Which type of representation would you prefer for your company? Do you think the investment involved in direct manufacture or distribution is worthwhile? Why?/Why not?
b What powers would you give to an agent abroad, and what restrictions would you want to put on his or her work?
c Do you think governments should make laws which limit foreign participation in the business of their country, or limit the repatriation of profits? What are the pros and cons of these restrictions?

8 WRITING

a Write a letter to the buying house of a famous American mail order company, describing your latest product, and saying why they should consider buying it for the American market.
b Imagine you are starting to sell to a new country, and you have a new agent in that country. Write a letter telling the agent what you expect him or her to do for your business.

LEGAL PUBLISHING & CONFERENCES DIVISION,
16-17 BRIDE LANE, LONDON, EC4Y 8EB
Telephone: 01-353 1000
Telegrams: Lloydslist LondonEC3 Telex: 987321 Lloyds G
Registered Office: Lloyd's, Lime Street, London, EC3M 7HA

Your Reference:—

Our Reference:—

ADVANCE NOTICE
55-YEAR CONSOLIDATED INDEX TO LLOYD'S LAW REPORTS

Lloyd's Law Reports were first published in October, 1919, under the title "Lloyd's List Law Reports". The early reports were reprints of law reports published in Lloyd's List. From 1935 verbatim judgments were published in the series, which is now the oldest series of law reports specialising in maritime and commercial cases. Digests of the cases reported have been published at approximately 5-year intervals, but these digests now number 14 so research through Lloyd's Law Reports may be difficult. Having received many requests for a consolidated index to the series, the publishers are now pleased to announce plans to produce a 6-volume consolidated index.

Vol. 1: Maritime Arbitration, Charter-parties (Time and Voyage), Sale of Ship.

Vol. 2: Bill of Lading, Cargo and Carriage by Sea.

Vol. 3: Marine Insurance, General Average and Salvage.

Vol. 4: Arrest, Detention, Collision, Lien, Negligence and Ship Management.

Vol. 5: Berth, Docks and Ports, Lighterage, Pilotage, Ship's Agent and Towage.

Vol. 6: International Sales Contracts and Sale of Goods (c.i.f. and f.o.b.), Principal and Agent.

Each volume will be supplemented with a table of contents, names of ships and words and phrases judicially considered, and, where relevant, a table of commodities.

The price for Volume 1 in this series (planned publication date: December, 1980) will be £35, but orders received before the end of October, 1980, from existing subscribers to Lloyd's **legal** publications will be fulfilled at the special price of £25.

The publication dates and prices of the further volumes in the series will be available in early 1981. Enquiries and orders should be addressed to:

Geoffrey Hall,
16/17 Bride Lane,
London, E.C.4.

Telephone: 01-353 1000
Telex: 987321 Lloyds G.

REGISTERED NUMBER   1072954 ENGLAND

Chairman: A C Sturge M.C. Managing Director: C W Welch Directors: C T G Blackmore, B J Brennan, M.C., K J Lambert Coles, A B Gray, S M Herbert, C A Thomas

The above circular is reproduced with permission of Lloyd's of London Press Ltd.

A Look at these sections before you read the text:

1 VOCABULARY

consolidated index index that brings all the other indexes together
verbatim written down exactly as it was spoken
maritime involving the sea
digest summary
intervals periods of time between two things happening
judicially carefully

2 SKIM

a What are Lloyd's publishing this year?
b In what way is this product new and different?

Now read the text and answer the skim questions.

B Look at these sections after reading the text:

3 COMPREHENSION

a What is Lloyd's business? What do they sell?
b How long have the verbatim reports been published?
c What are the reports about?
d Why is it necessary to publish a new index?
e How many books of summaries of law reports have Lloyd's published?

4 INFERENCE

a Why is it necessary to publish the *verbatim* reports of legal cases?
b Why would research be difficult without the new consolidated index?
c Which words and phrases in each volume would be 'judicially considered'? Why are they put into each volume of the index?

5 REFERENCE

a What is Lloyd's List?
b What does f.o.b. mean?
c What does EC4Y 8EB in the address refer to? What is it called?

6 LANGUAGE

Each business has its own jargon, and this text contains jargon from the shipping and shipping insurance businesses, such as *lien*. Find out what this means, and then look at the following words. They are all formed in the same way, and so they can be easily understood. For example:
*carri**age*** = the act of carrying something somewhere
or, the cost of carrying something somewhere
Find out what these words ending in -*age* mean:
salvage lighterage pilotage towage

7 OPINION

a What sort of research do you think people want to do with Lloyd's Law Reports? Would they be useful in your work?
b Why are the reports offered more cheaply to people who order before a certain date? Is there any advantage in this for Lloyd's?
c Do you think many people will want to buy these indexes? Is this a profitable business? How many copies would you estimate could be sold?

8 WRITING

a Summarise the product offered in this letter in a memo to your Shipping Manager. Ask if this might be useful or not.
b Write to Lloyd's, placing an official order for the Index, and enquire when Volume 3 (insurance) will be available. Write a very formal letter.

And now, the Three-Orange-Juice BREAKFAST

If you're in business, breakfast might be your most important meal of the day. (Just what Mother always told you)

By Peter Andrews

If the law is a jealous mistress, Wall Street is a live-in girl friend who never lets you out of her sight. Demanding, unceasing and unremitting, the business requires more and more time just to get the job done until there is hardly any time at all left in the day just for fun. Lunch, whether it be with two Perriers or with President Carter's dreaded three martinis, has been a hard-nosed affair where the deal always counted for more than the ravigotte ever since Delmonico's first introduced the concept of the business lunch in the early nineteenth century. Dinner, with its late-night skull sessions where the contracts come out with the mints, has been shot for years now. Until a few years ago, the only mealtime a Wall Streeter could call his own was breakfast – when he could come to the table in a dressing gown, punch down a bit of fruit juice and snarl at the children.

But now, even that respite is gone. Breakfast, a semicivilized meal at the best of times, has become for many top Wall Street executives just another business appointment in an already crowded calendar. At New York's midtown Brasserie restaurant, which is open 24 hours a day, the last of the Broadway denizens are barely out

the door in the early morning when the brokers take over the booths along the walls to map out strategy for the day to come. A few blocks uptown, by 8:00 A.M., the limousines are parked two deep on Park Avenue in front of the Regency Hotel – where investment bankers from many a firm brave cold coffee and colder service to begin forging deals before the traditional start of the business day. Clubs such as the Links and the Brook, where the morning hush used to be only rarely broken by anything more serious than the sound of a hasty hangover cure in the works, now reverberate with a brisk breakfast trade. And at banks such as Morgan Guaranty, the first sound of day is not the comforting rustle of greenbacks in the counting rooms, but the clatter of chafing dishes serving up scrambled eggs.

For better or worse – and there are many who will say it is very much for the worse – breakfast is now an official part of the Wall Street business day. In point of fact, breakfast – rather than lunch or dinner – is now the time when many bankers and brokers accomplish their most hard-nosed wheeling and dealing. "Investment banking breakfasts tend to be more business-oriented," says George Ball, president of E.F. Hutton. "They're conversational, but they deal with specific problems." The talk at breakfast, adds another banker, is more direct "because both sides want to get to the office," and is not slowed down with the social amenities of a business lunch or dinner. "When people drink, they tend to chit-chat," he sniffs. "When they have coffee and juice, they can get right down to it."

But the most important phenomenon that has been elevating breakfast into a deal-making institution is geography. By no small coincidence, many of the major firms that have moved to midtown Manhattan – such as Smith Barney, Morgan Stanley, Lazard Freres and Blyth Eastman Dillon among them – are the biggest users of breakfast meetings. One reason is that the midtown area has more places that serve up decent eggs and the proper atmosphere. But more importantly, the time-consuming lunchtime trek from uptown to downtown, or vice versa, is a luxury that investment executives can ill afford. With transportation factored in, figures Dreyfus chairman Howard Stein, lunch can eat up 2½ valuable business hours. "And you have to adjust your mind for going out to lunch and coming back, which takes another half hour," adds Stein. "So that's three hours out of the day."

ILLUSTRATION BY STEVEN GUARNACCIA

A Look at these sections before you read the text:

1 VOCABULARY

mistress lover
live-in living in the same house
unremitting never stopping
dreaded feared
hard-nosed unsentimental; unemotional
ravigotte name of a French meal
skull session talking and discussing
(to) snarl (to) talk angrily

Now read the text and answer the skim questions.

2 SKIM

a Why are businesspeople having breakfast together?
b Where is the service very 'cold'?
c Which restaurant is open 24 hours a day?

B Look at these sections after reading the text:

3 COMPREHENSION

a Who first introduced the business lunch?
b Where are the limousines parked in the early morning?
c What do businesspeople think about the business breakfast?
d What makes breakfast meetings quicker than lunch meetings?

4 INFERENCE

a Why is dinner not interesting any more?
b Why is it easier to discuss business at breakfast, and not take a long time in social conversation?
c What makes breakfast 'a semicivilised meal at the best of times'?

5 REFERENCE

a What is Perrier?
b Who are the 'Broadway denizens'?
c What is the difference between uptown, midtown and downtown?

6 LANGUAGE

Look at this sentence from the text:
*Demanding, **unceasing** and **unremitting**, the business . . .*
These are complicated words for the simple idea *not stopping*. The writer uses these words to give the text some style. He also uses idiomatic words and phrases in the same way.
Try to find the words and phrases in the text which have these meanings:

a rest, quiet time
b to echo, make a noise
c to need
d to create, make
e to achieve
f useless, no good
g drink quickly
h to plan
i dollar banknotes
j negotiating and discussing

7 OPINION

a Why should businesspeople have to work at breakfast time? Would you do this regularly?
b The text says there is no more time left in the day 'just for fun'. Is this true? Do you think businesspeople work too hard?
c Why is Wall Street compared to a 'girlfriend'? What does this tell you about the business world?

8 WRITING

a You want to discuss an important deal with a client. Write an invitation to breakfast. Explain where you can meet, and why it's a good idea.
b Write a report for your Managing Director, explaining how much money can be saved by having breakfast meetings rather than lunchtime meetings. Suggest that your company starts to serve breakfast in the executive dining room.

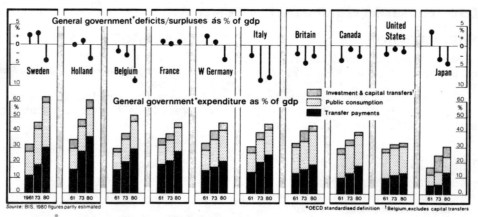

The rise and rise of the public sector

Source: BIS, 1980 figures partly estimated

*OECD standardised definition †Belgium, excludes capital transfers

Governments in most industrial countries are trying to trim the size of their public spending. And finding it damnably difficult, for three reasons:

● Slow economic growth. Since the 1979 oil price shock, Opec's current account surplus has risen by $110 billion; the deflationary effect on western economies has boosted both unemployment and industrial subsidies.

● Demography. The number of pension-age dependants has risen nearly everywhere, both absolutely and as a proportion of the population.

● Indexation. Many transfer payments—pensions, unemployment pay, etc—are indexed to inflation, so if an economy is actually contracting (eg, Britain's in 1980-81) their share of gdp is bound to rise. Higher transfers accounted for more than half the growth in spending between 1961 and 1980 in the countries shown in our chart. In America, public consumption actually fell as a proportion of gdp, while transfers increased their share from 8.8% to 12.7% of gdp over the same period.

Spending and deficits are not always related: Japan had one of the biggest budget deficits in the OECD (4% of gdp) in 1980, and one of the smallest public sectors (32%). But the desire to cut fiscal deficits is one reason why governments are keen to cut public spending. The alternative is to raise taxes—politically unpopular at the best of times, but especially when real incomes are squeezed by slow growth.

So how do governments go about making cuts? Answer: the easy way. Transfers are hard to reduce because they are tied to political and moral ideals about equity: why hit the old and the unemployed when they are already disadvantaged? Cutting public consumption is tricky when it involves destroying civil servants' empires.

So government axemen often go first for public investment programmes, involving only the cancellation of a few contracts with private companies. By the time the sewers start leaking and the roads have potholes, some other government will have to take the blame.

A Look at these sections before you read the text:

1 VOCABULARY

(to) trim (to) reduce; (to) cut
damnably difficult very difficult
demography the study of population
indexation connecting pay rises with price rises
axemen economists looking for budgets which they can cut
sewers pipes under the street carrying dirty water
potholes holes in the road

Now read the text and answer the skim questions.

2 SKIM

a Does the article think the rise of the public sector is good or bad?
b Which country has the biggest deficit?

B Look at these sections after reading the text:

3 COMPREHENSION

a What was the shock of 1979? What was its effect on the West?
b How has Western population changed its structure?
c What is a transfer payment?
d What problems are caused by indexation of transfer payments?
e What is the alternative to cutting public spending, according to the article?

4 INFERENCE

a What is meant by 'civil servants' empires'? Why should making spending cuts be difficult?
b The article suggests that 'by the time the sewers start leaking . . . some other government will have to take the blame'. What does this mean? Does the writer of the article think all governments are short-sighted?

5 REFERENCE

a Find out what OPEC and OECD mean in English.
b What are the words summarised by gdp?
c What could the letters BIS refer to—especially as they are connected to the information in the chart?

6 LANGUAGE

Look at this sentence from the text:
Cutting public consumption is tricky, when . . .
This is a more interesting way of saying:
It is tricky to cut public consumption, when . . .
Now re-write these sentences to make them more interesting:

a It is difficult to reduce public spending, when transfers are increasing.
b It is hard to stop the indexation of transfers, for political reasons.
c It is easier to cancel contracts with private companies.
d It is unpopular to raise taxes, especially at a time like this.
e It is a long job to trim the size of government spending.

7 OPINION

a What do you think is the cause of the demographic changes in the world? What long-term effect will this have?
b From the information in the chart, which country do you think is in the worst situation? What reasons can you see for this?
c Can you suggest any other alternatives to cutting budget deficits? Which policy would you prefer?
d Do you think it is important to get rid of budget deficits? Can a government afford to keep a budget deficit over a long period of time?

8 WRITING

a Using the information given in the chart, write a comparison of the economic situation of five countries, explaining what has happened since 1963.
b Imagine you are a government economist. You must advise the president or prime minister on future economic policy in your own country. What advice would you give? Write a short summary of the policies that you would suggest.

Retailing

Thorny question of discounts

Britain's Christmas shoppers did not find Rolex watches, Dunlop tennis racquets, Dorma beds, or 28 other product lines in Argos catalogue showrooms. Tesco customers may note the absence of Thorn's Ferguson brand televisions and audio equipment. According to Tesco and Argos, these and other manufacturers are refusing to supply price-cutting retailers. The Office of Fair Trading (OFT) is now investigating the two companies' separate complaints.

This is the most recent battle in a 15-year war since the law was changed to forbid manufacturers to impose recommended retail prices as a condition of supply. The OFT receives about 30 such documented complaints a year (34 in 1979), as well as "several complaints a day" from retailers unwilling or unable to follow through with evidence.

Manufacturers say they do not want their products marketed through retail outlets which do not provide adequate pre-sale advice or after-sale service. They cannot supply discounters, they say, because that would drive independent dealers, who do provide such service, out of business.

Some manufacturers (including Thorn) are willing to sell discounters other product lines, or similar ones sold under a second, less well-known brand name. Discounters reply that consumers should have the choice between low prices and fancy service. They say that manufacturers are just dressing up resale price maintenance.

OFT officials are keen to pursue the charges, but the chances that they will pin anything on, for instance, Thorn are remote. Since 1964, with hundreds of complaints to act on, the OFT has secured several undertakings from offending manufacturers and brought only one case to court (Comet's case against Hotpoint in mid-1979). In that one case, the parties promptly settled out of court.

Discount retailers say the OFT is weedy. The OFT justly replies that the narrowly-drawn Resale Prices Act makes it next to impossible to bring a court-worthy case. It must prove that the desire to fix resale prices was not just a major motive but the sole motive for the refusal to supply. Since the OFT has almost no fact-finding powers in these cases and most marketing contacts are made by telephone anyway, this already heavy burden of proof is even heavier to discharge.

The government's new competition bill came out of committee last week and is expected to become law in February. It should make the OFT's job easier—in theory. The act gives the OFT broad authority (too broad, critics say) to investigate any anti-competitive practice and the power to demand documents. The Liesner committee report on restrictive practices last March said this approach was best suited to solving most resale price problems.

Others doubt whether so fuzzily-worded a concept as "anti-competitive practice" will stand up against the sharply-defined provisions of the Resale Prices Act. Many discounters are not unhappy that the power to enforce supply should remain the vague threat which it now is in the competition bill. There is no law made which a clever man cannot and will not get round, they say. Were the OFT to force Rolex, for instance, to supply Argos, the watchmakers could well find ways of delaying or confusing deliveries. In the real world, a contract still demands a willing seller and a willing buyer.

A Look at these sections before you read the text:

1 VOCABULARY

thorny difficult
retailer person or company selling to the public
adequate good enough
dressing up making something seem more attractive than it is
(to) pursue (to) chase after; (to) follow; *here*, (to) investigate
(to) pin . . . on somebody (to) blame somebody for something
weedy weak
burden of proof responsibility to find proof

Now read the text and answer the skim questions.

2 SKIM

a What are Tesco and Argos complaining about?
b What is the government's new law on this matter? What will it do?

B Look at these sections after reading the text:

3 COMPREHENSION

a Which manufacturers will not supply Tesco with products?
b Why will the manufacturers not supply Argos or Tesco?
c What does the law say about this? Is it legal to refuse to sell your products to a company that sells them cheaply?
d What does the Office of Fair Trading do about these problems?
e Why are these cases hard to prove?

4 INFERENCE

a Why does the Office of Fair Trading appear to be so weak?
b Why are the manufacturers unhappy with these discount retailers? Do they make more profit from sales to 'ordinary' shops and retailers?
c Why is the phrase 'anti-competitive practice' described as 'fuzzily-worded'? Is it not clear what the government wants to do?
d How could the manufacturers find ways of 'delaying or confusing deliveries'? What could they do?

5 REFERENCE

a Find out what Argos and Tesco mean to British readers. What are they famous for?
b What are Hotpoint and Comet? Which one is the manufacturer?

6 LANGUAGE

Look at this sentence from the text:
   Were the OFT **to force** Rolex to supply Argos, the watchmakers could find. . . .
This is a more formal, and more interesting, way of saying:
   If the OFT forc**ed** Rolex to supply Argos. . . .
Now re-write these sentences using the *were to* + infinitive form:

a If the OFT took Dunlop to court, they could make them supply Tesco and Argos.
b If Tesco raised its prices, Ferguson would perhaps supply them.
c If Tesco and Argos won their case, the consumers would be very happy.
d If the prices fell much lower, the independent dealers would be forced out of business.

7 OPINION

a Why does the government try to make laws about business practices? Should there be any limits to trading?
b What are the advantages of resale price maintenance? Who gets most benefit from fixed retail prices?
c Which company would you support—the manufacturer or the retailer?
d Is this problem only found in Britain? What is the situation concerning retail prices in your country?

8 WRITING

a Imagine you are a discount retailer who cannot get products from a large manufacturer. Write to the Managing Director of the manufacturing company and complain about this policy. Explain why you feel the company should supply you.
b Explain in a memo your own company's policy on price controls and supplying discounters.

How to Do It Better

The concept, born in the late 1940s, seemed remarkably simple: put together small teams of labor and management people in a nonhierarchical setting, ask them to spot and solve problems on the production line—and presto, they would achieve greater efficiency and higher quality. Like dozens of ideas "Made in America," the notion of the "quality circle" first found widespread acceptance in Japan, where major manufacturers have been using it with undeniable success for more than two decades. Now the QC is coming home. In recent years, about 150 American companies, including General Motors, Ford, Westinghouse and Bethlehem Steel, have set up quality circles, and most have found their employees to be valuable new sources of money-saving ideas. Says L. J. Hudspeth, Westinghouse's vice president for corporate productivity: "They know more about operations than you do."

New Skills: A quality circle is typically made up of eight to twelve volunteer workers and supervisors. They receive several hours of training on how to gather and use data—skills they will need to find solutions to sticky problems. The circle then meets weekly on company time, hashing over problems members encounter on the job. Worthy suggestions on how to improve operations are passed on to higher management, which has two weeks to accept or reject them.

The acceptance rate is high—and the results at times rather striking. A QC at Northrop, for instance, was troubled because bits used to drill holes in titanium for F-5 fighter planes kept breaking. Solution: change the drilling angle and specify bits made from harder steel. Since it was adopted, the proposal has saved Northrop $70,000 in lost time. A worker-management team at the General Motors assembly plant in Tarrytown, N.Y., may actually have prevented the big facility from closing, says Irving Bluestone, a recently retired United Auto Workers vice president. In the early 1970s, the plant was plagued by violence and absenteeism. The quality of its cars was poor and each year employees filed 2,500 to 3,000 grievances. Then the workers were brought into the decision-making process. GM won't discuss what happened in detail, but grievances fell sharply—to about 40 a year—and the plant got a solid lease on life when the company decided to use it to produce its highly successful X cars. Ford Motor recently adopted a variation on the QC theme. It gave 48 hours of special training to workers at the two plants that are now producing Ford's entrants into the economy-car sweepstakes, the Ford Escort and Mercury Lynx. Ford hopes the teams will be able to spot start-up problems on the assembly line, saving the company grief later on.

A quality circle meets at Northrop: Big payoffs from a twice-borrowed idea

Bart Photo

Rewards: Some companies reward good ideas handsomely. Northrop, for instance, passes on 10 per cent of any dollar savings to the quality circle that comes up with the suggestion—and the team decides how to divvy up the money among its members. But most companies say the employee's biggest reward is the feeling of involvement. "What we are appealing to is people's desire for recognition by their peers," says Phil Shapiro, who coordinates the QC program at Northrop. "They appreciate the opportunity to participate." Some critics discard the whole notion of the quality circle as nothing but a dressed-up suggestion box. But more and more companies seem to find it another useful tool in promoting productivity.

DAVID PAULY with JOSEPH CONTRERAS
in Los Angeles and WILLIAM D. MARBACH
in Detroit

A Look at these sections before you read the text:

1 VOCABULARY

nonhierarchical not organised according to grades or levels in the company
setting situation
(to) spot (to) see; (to) find out
presto *here*, immediately
notion idea
decade 10 years
sticky difficult
(to) divvy up (to) divide up; (to) share

Now read the text and answer the skim questions.

2 SKIM

a Who has recently introduced quality circles into their company?
b Where were quality circles first successful?

B Look at these sections after reading the text:

3 COMPREHENSION

a Where and when did the idea of the quality circle start?
b What is a quality circle? Who is in it?
c What results do quality circles usually have?
d What were the results at Northrop?

4 INFERENCE

a Why has the idea only recently become popular in the USA?
b Why will General Motors not discuss what happened in their quality circles?
c What could have been the cause of the 'violence and absenteeism' at the General Motors assembly plant in Tarrytown? Why did it suddenly disappear?

5 REFERENCE

a QC obviously means quality circle—but it wouldn't usually be used in Britain. Why not? What does QC traditionally refer to in the UK?
b What does NY refer to?
c What do you understand by 'United Auto Workers'?
d What sort of company is Northrop? How can you tell?

6 LANGUAGE

Look at this sentence from the text:
About 150 American companies . . . have **set up** *quality circles . . .*
The meaning of phrasal verbs, like this, is not always clear from the verb alone. *Set up*, in this context, means 'started' or 'organised'. Try to find the phrasal and prepositional verbs in the text that have these meanings:
a composed of, it consists of
b sent to, given to
c thinks of, originates
d discussing, thinking about

7 OPINION

a Why do you think these circles are successful? Is it because of the money the members of the circles might receive?
b Do you agree with L J Hudson of Westinghouse that employees 'know more about operations than you do'? Who does he mean by 'you' in this sentence?
c Would you recommend the use of quality circles in your company? Why?/Why not?

8 WRITING

a Write a memo for your Board of Directors suggesting that the American quality circle should be introduced into your company. Explain what the advantages would be, and estimate the money that could be saved.
b Imagine you are in a quality circle. What suggestions would you make to improve the efficiency of your company? Write your suggestions as a report.

BRITAIN : SALESMANSHIP 'THE WEAKEST LINK'

Just back from the salesman's funeral?

BY MARTIN VAN MESDAG

A FEW DAYS ago I learnt that, for its sales conference, a motor vehicle company had chosen as its theme: "The Return to Selling."

If my own experience is anything to go by, the company concerned must be unique in its industry both for its implicit admission of having neglected selling, and for its wisdom in seeking to do something about it.

British salesmanship is in a sorry state — if not in absolute terms, then certainly in comparison with the salesmanship of foreign competitors.

Countries which are our biggest export customers enjoy much higher shares of our imports than we do of their's, so that whether our industries sell at home or abroad, they are confronted by international competition.

Next to poor compliance with delivery commitments, salesmanship is seen to be the weakest link in our competitive performance, as recent research makes clear.

Earlier this year, the Sussex University Science Policy Research Unit reported on a series of surveys of failures in industrial innovation.

According to the Unit's senior Fellow, Roy Rothwell: "Britain's inability to keep pace with the steady development of technology, coupled with lack of attention to marketing needs, is the reason for our national decline." He added that Germany's "sales and marketing bias" had a lot to do with her success in engineering.

More recently, an Institute of Marketing report, Purchasing Industrial Goods from British Suppliers, published this month, found that the main weaknesses in the sales efforts mounted by British suppliers were as follows: inadequate knowledge of customers' needs; poor communication between sales and all other company departments; and a low level of business-generating activity, notably in the more traditional industry sectors.

Here are some chilling quotations from the Institute's report:

" . . . salesmen tend not only to be badly trained, but the service provided by (their) companies is generally bad . . . The performance of many sales forces can clearly be improved."

" . . . all too often, visiting salesmen would have little or no idea whether production could be stretched to meet new orders."

" . . . salesmen failed to understand their own products, and did not have sufficient technical expertise to be able to adapt their products to customers' needs."

"Salesmen washed their hands of orders once they were booked."

"Buyers always had to go out and actively seek sources of supply in Britain, whereas

> ' In many cases, a company's poor sales performance is part and parcel of a generally underdeveloped marketing awareness. But I suspect there are also cases of companies whose product development, advertising, promotion and research effort are up to scratch, but who neglect the sharp end of marketing: selling.'

foreign companies actively promoted and sold their products.'

The report went on to show that such shortcoming were far less often displayed by non-British suppliers.

Reporting on a large-scale survey among purchasing managers of British companies a few months ago, the Institute of Purchasing and Supply provided an evaluation of the performance of suppliers' salesmen. It revealed that inadequate negotiating skills and insufficient knowledge of customers' businesses were seen to be salesmen's greatest weaknesses.

The salesman's inadequate knowledge of the market environment in which he and his products are competing is confirmed by other research.

For example, last year AGS Management Consultants of Singapore surveyed a sample of business managers in Singapore, Malaysia and Hong Kong, and obtained a rating of British salesmen against their rivals from other countries.

While British salesmen's diplomacy and honesty were highly rated, they came bottom on "perseverance" and "thoroughness of preparation."

It is not a pretty picture.

We hear moans from the Government and the unions about the need for increased investment in industry, from the Government and the management organisations about the need for greater productivity, and from all three about the need for a greater R&D effort.

But isn't it possible that the facts point to much more obvious and straightforward remedies for some of our ills?

The research findings already quoted implicate not so much the salesmen themselves as their managers, and those who manage their companies.

In many cases, as the research suggests, a company's poor sales performance is part and parcel of a generally underdeveloped marketing awareness. But I suspect there are also cases of companies whose product development, advertising, promotion and research effort are up to scratch, but who neglect the sharp end of marketing: selling.

In my view, the emergence of concepts like account management, physical distribution management, and trade marketing, have come about as palliatives for the neglect or downgrading of selling.

As I see it, the rapid increase in the competitiveness of foreign suppliers, both in home and overseas markets, and the concentration of buying power found in many of the markets in which we sell, call for more, rather than less, emphasis on selling.

Our salesmen need to be trained and managed if they are to become skilled neogtiators; if they are to become and remain knowledgeable about their customers' trading environments, and if they are to persevere in efforts to service existing business as well as generate new business.

Salesmen's tasks need to become an integral part of the organisation, known and understood by all as the "front end."

It is indeed time for a "return to selling."

Martin van Mesdag is a marketing consultant.

A Look at these sections before you read the text:

1 VOCABULARY

implicit not said directly
in a sorry state in a bad situation
compliance keeping to an agreement
innovation introduction of new ideas
coupled with joined to
mounted organised (of sales campaigns)
chilling frightening
perseverance quality of following an aim to the end

Now read the text and answer the skim questions.

2 SKIM

a What is the problem with Britain's salesmen?
b Who has done research on this problem?

B Look at these sections after reading the text:

3 COMPREHENSION

a What was special about the motor vehicle company?
b What is the other big problem of British industry?
c In what ways are other countries different?
d What problems do British salesmen have? Give three from the text.
e How do British salesmen compare with salesmen from other countries?

4 INFERENCE

a What is the 'salesman's funeral'? What does the writer mean?
b Why is 'The Return to Selling' a good theme? What does the writer think most companies have failed to do?
c In what way is the selling problem connected to a marketing problem?
d How do the research findings 'implicate not so much the salesmen . . . as their managers'? What is the fault of the managers?

5 REFERENCE

a What does the Science Policy Research Unit do?
b What is a senior Fellow?

6 LANGUAGE

Look at this sentence from the text:
British salesmanship is in a sorry state.
This is quite a colloquial or idiomatic phrase—the informal language of spoken discussion. Try and find idioms and phrases in the text, that have the following, rather formal, meanings:
a refused responsibility for
b are a good indication of the situation
c up to the necessary standard
d a normal part of
e it is not a good impression

7 OPINION

a Do you think the author is too pessimistic about Britain's salesmen? If so, does he prove that he is right?
b Do you think Britain has a reputation for bad delivery performance as well as bad salesmanship? What are your experiences of British industry?
c What do you think are the most important qualities of a good salesman? What makes one person successful and another not successful?
d What do you think is the real difference between marketing and selling? Why is selling called 'the sharp end of marketing' in the article?

8 WRITING

a Write a report on the sales force in your company, explaining their good and bad qualities, and suggesting how they could improve their work.
b Imagine you have been asked to give a paper, on the art of selling, at an international conference. Write a draft of your talk.

PERSONAL SERVICES-6
COMPANY FORMATION AND MANAGEMENT

There are many uses for a Jersey or Guernsey Company. Because Barclaytrust International is part of the Barclays Group with connections in Europe and overseas, we are well placed to be of maximum help and provide information and advice quickly and efficiently.

We can arrange for the incorporation of companies under the laws of Jersey and Guernsey and provide corporate and administrative services to run them.

Our services include:
1. Maintaining the statutory registered office of the Company.

2. Providing Nominee shareholders.

3. Providing the Company Secretary, Directors and other Officers.

4. Maintaining the statutory records of the Company, keeping the Minutes of Directors and Shareholders' meetings and making the necessary returns.

5. Keeping full accounting records and preparing the accounts for audit.

Most companies set up in this way are beneficially owned by individuals resident outside the Channel Islands.

Tax Advantages

The companies which are owned by residents of Jersey and Guernsey or operate in Jersey or Guernsey, are liable to pay income tax at the rate of 20% per annum on their profits. However, there is a provision in the law allowing companies which are owned by non-residents of either Island, which do not operate within the Islands and whose management lies outside both Islands, to pay Corporation Tax of £300 per annum maximum instead of Income Tax. Companies whose profits do not exceed £1,500 in any one year may opt to pay income tax at the rate of 20%. If a company is paying Jersey or Guernsey income tax, the Authorities will require the filing of accounts to substantiate the assessable profit. However, provided a company opts to pay the Corporation Tax of £300 per annum and fulfills the criteria for being granted 'Corporation Tax' status, it is not required to file accounts.

Barclaytrust arranges to take advantage of the Corporation Tax Law for companies where the owners are resident outside Jersey and Guernsey and the company does not carry on business in Jersey or Guernsey, by establishing the Board of Directorship in such a way that the majority of directors are neither resident in Jersey or Guernsey. Board meetings of such companies are usually held in Sark, where there is no income tax, ensuring that the company enjoys the Corporation Tax status from the Jersey or Guernsey authorities, but does not incur tax liabilities by operating from any other country.

Fees and Expenses

For the provision of routine administration and management services for the company, including the provision of nominee shareholders and directors, Registered Office, Secretary, holding the Annual General Meeting of the company, preparing simple accounts of the company and filing the company's tax return ... £500 per annum.

Other services rendered to companies including work undertaken in setting up a company are charged for on a 'time-spent' basis.

An annual registration fee of £50 is payable to the States of Jersey or Guernsey as appropriate.

Any expenses or disbursements, including any directors fees payable, incurred on behalf of the company, will be charged to the company.

Incorporation Costs

The cost of registering and incorporating a company in Jersey or Guernsey with an authorised capital of £5,000 or its equivalent in any currency is about £400. This sum includes legal costs, registration fee, the provision of the company's name-plate and Seal, registers, share certificates, etc. Stamp Duty is charged on authorised capital at the rate of ½% (minimum £25).

A Look at these sections before you read the text:

1 VOCABULARY

well placed in a good situation
incorporation forming of a company
statutory necessary according to the law
minutes written record of a meeting
returns declarations of income
beneficially owned owned for the benefit of . . .
(to) opt (to) choose
(to) substantiate (to) prove

Now read the text and answer the skim questions.

2 SKIM

a What service is Barclays Bank offering?
b How is it possible to keep your accounts secret?

B Look at these sections after reading the text:

3 COMPREHENSION

a What is the cost of using the Bank's services, per year?
b How much must the company pay to the government of Jersey or Guernsey, if the owner lives in Jersey or Guernsey?
c How can a company pay only corporation tax and not income tax? What are the conditions?
d How much capital must a new company have, as a minimum?

4 INFERENCE

a Why must the directors be resident outside Jersey or Guernsey?
b When will it be better for a company to choose to pay income tax instead of corporation tax?

5 REFERENCE

a Where are the islands of Jersey and Guernsey? Who controls them?
b What does a nominee shareholder refer to?
c What is the usual difference between income tax and corporation tax?
d What and where is Sark?
e What could Stamp Duty refer to?

6 LANGUAGE

Look at this sentence from the text:
*Our services include **maintaining** the statutory registered office of the company.*
Another way of saying this, without using the -*ing* form, is:
*Our services include **the maintenance of** the statutory registered office of the company.*
Try and find the nouns that could replace the -*ing* form in these sentences:
Our services include:
a providing directors for the company.
b paying the annual fee to the government.
c arranging the tax affairs of the company.
d preparing the annual accounts of the company.
e registering the name of the company.

7 OPINION

a Why should a person living outside Jersey want to start a company there? Is there any advantage over other countries like Switzerland, Liechtenstein, for example?
b Why should the government of Jersey be so generous to companies? Why do you think they do not have higher taxes?
c Would there be any benefit for your company if it was incorporated in Jersey? If so, what would it be?

8 WRITING

a Write a letter to Barclaytrust International asking for more details of how you can set up your own company, and how much it would cost you.
b Write a memo to the Finance Director of your company, suggesting the formation of a company in Jersey or Guernsey. Ask for his or her thoughts on this suggestion.

About Hewlett-Packard

Compact and unobtrusive in office setting, Hewlett-Packard HP 3000 Series 40 supports multiple terminals, printers, and other peripherals.

Hewlett-Packard began as a small company in 1939 in Palo Alto, California. William Hewlett and David Packard, two Stanford University graduate engineers, built their first product, a resistance-capacity audio oscillator, with an original investment of $538. This oscillator was easier to use, more stable, and less expensive than others available at the time. The first sale was to a Walt Disney Studios engineer who was impressed enough by the oscillator to order eight to be used in filming the movie "Fantasia."

With this modest start, the company grew in its first ten years from annual sales of $5,000 to $2 million and a total of 200 employees. By 1959, an expanding product line of electronic test and measurement instruments produced sales of $66,577,000 and employment was 2,378.

In the 1960's the demand for increasingly sophisticated electronic equipment led to the development of the first Hewlett-Packard minicomputer. This original model, announced in 1966, was designed to interface easily with test and measurement instruments and thus make them more efficient and accurate. The success of this specialized computer naturally pointed the way to customer requirements for small, powerful computers adaptable to a variety of jobs. Until the mid-1960's most computers had been expensive, large-scale systems, so the HP 2000 time-sharing systems introduced in 1968 found a ready market and quickly established the company as a leading producer of minicomputers. By the end of the 60's decade, the total corporate sales were $367 million.

Through continued growth in the 1970's, Hewlett-Packard today is a major manufacturer of electronic equipment for measurement and computation with sales of 4.25 billion, divided about 50% domestic and 50% international. For the past four years, electronic data products sales have increased 31% per year, and are approximately 51% of total sales.

More than 4,700 different products are manufactured and marketed by Hewlett-Packard. Major product categories encompass electronic test and measuring instruments, solid-state components, electronic calculators, medical electronic products, electronic instrumentation for chemical analysis, and computers. The company employs 67,000 people at 32 U.S. divisions, 14 overseas plants, and sales and service facilities throughout the world.

This is an excerpt from Hewlett-Packard's annual report.

A Look at these sections before you read the text:

1 VOCABULARY

stable unchanging; reliable
movie film
exceeded was bigger than
sophisticated complicated and advanced
(to) interface (to) connect
computation calculation using computers
(to) encompass (to) include
solid-state transistorised electronics

2 SKIM

a Who started the company? How much money did they start with?
b What sort of business does it do now?

Now read the text and answer the skim questions.

B Look at these sections after reading the text:

3 COMPREHENSION

a What was Hewlett-Packard's first product? Who was their first customer?
b What new products did they develop in the 1960s?
c How much of their business is international?
d Where was the company's first base?
e Where does the name of the company come from?

4 INFERENCE

a Why was Hewlett-Packard's first product so successful?
b What was so important about Hewlett-Packard's development of the HP 2000 in 1968?
c What is the major growth product group for Hewlett-Packard?

5 REFERENCE

a Where is Stanford University? What is it famous for?
b What is Walt Disney famous for?

6 LANGUAGE

Look at this sentence from the text:
> The engineer **was impressed enough** by the oscillator **to order** eight. . . .

This is another way of saying:
> The engineer was so impressed by the oscillator that he ordered eight.

Now re-write these sentences in the same way:
a The company was so successful that it built a new plant.
b The sales were so good that they justified new staff.
c The profits were so high that they allowed an extra dividend.
d The board was so impressed by the staff's work that they gave them a 15% pay increase.
e The product was so cheap that it destroyed the competition.

7 OPINION

a The company has grown from an investment of $538 to a billion dollar business in only 45 years. Is this faster or slower growth than most companies? What sort of skills are necessary to organise and control a company so that it grows like this?
b Could you start a company with only $538 investment? What sort of business would you start, and how would you do it?
c When a company employs 40,000 people in 40 different places, it is not easy to know everything that is happening in the company. Is it possible for the people who started the company to keep control over such a large number of people? Is it always a good idea to let the company grow so big—or should it be stopped at a certain size?

8 WRITING

a Write a short description of the history of your company—how it started, what happened to it over the years, and so on.
b Write a short text, for an advertising brochure, giving a profile of your company. Explain what it produces, the total sales, how many people are employed, where the plants are, and so on.

SITES AND PREMISES

Milton Keynes offers a wide range of sites and premises for industrialists. Companies that need to expand quickly to meet market demands can take advantage of the Development Corporation's offer to accept the surrender of factory leases when larger premises are being taken; it is also possible to reserve option sites for future development.

A diverse range of industry is established in Milton Keynes, including many small firms. Companies already familiar with the benefits of the city include Telephone Rentals, Hoechst, Burroughs, Scicon, Steinberg, General Motors, GEC-Marconi Avionics, Molins, Minolta, Scania (U.K.), Volkswagen, The Coca-Cola Export Corporation, Cole Plastics . . . the list could fill the page.

The choice of sites and premises includes campus sites with space for planning flexibility and future expansion; sites on which purpose-designed buildings can be constructed; and factory units ready for occupation – including groups of small factory units specially designed for newly-formed and growing businesses.

ADVANCE FACTORY UNITS

Advance factory units in Milton Keynes are industrial units built to high specifications ready for occupation by most kinds of manufacturing, service industry and warehousing. These factory units provide an ample supply of property in a range of sizes that will enable companies to move to the city and grow.

Factory units are being made available from 50 square metres (approximately 500 sq ft) to over 10,000 square metres (100,000 sq ft). More than 350 companies have taken such ready-built advance factory units in the last eight years. The building programme is now in excess of 50,000 square metres (500,000 sq ft) a year – a response to the ever-increasing interest and demand for the units.

The advance factory is a particularly practical proposition for those who do not want to tie up capital in land or buildings.

For smaller firms, they offer the most economical way to gain maximum use of space, together with the opportunity to expand into progressively larger units as business grows.

For larger firms, they can be used as efficient 'first stage' buildings. An advance factory unit can readily be established as a pilot plant, with little interruption to operations, while permanent, purpose-designed premises are completed on a nearby site.

SITES

Since 1970, more than 50 companies have taken sites throughout the city and, using either their own consultants or Development Corporation architects, have produced modern buildings varying widely in purpose and design.

Hoechst (UK) have built a centre for research, for example, while The Coca-Cola Export Corporation's plant fills hundreds of millions of cans of soft drinks every year (and their can supplier, Nacanco, has a new factory on the site next door). General Motors and Volkswagen both have new administrative, training and parts distribution centres. Cole Plastics have a superb new factory for compounding plastics and Newport Instruments were able to build a new factory for their electronics business at just a few months' notice. As each month passes, so more companies join the list.

Site lease development is particularly suited to the larger company with special requirements. In appropriate cases adjoining option land can be made available to cater for planned expansion. With option land available, a company need not make a full investment commitment until that is justified by the market for the company's products.

Of considerable importance to any company is the facility to step up the scale of operations at short notice. In Milton Keynes, when sudden unexpected surges in demand occur, a company can respond quickly by taking an advance factory unit temporarily while its factory extension is being completed.

Providing companies intend to take other sites or factory units in the city, the Development Corporation will readily accept the surrender of leases with no obligation on the company to find a new tenant. Since this scheme has been operating, many firms have expanded in this way – some of them more than once.

Details of the employment areas where sites and factories are available are given on the following pages.

A Look at these sections before you read the text:

1 VOCABULARY

premises factory or office space
diverse different
ample plenty of
pilot trial, experimental operation
adjoining next to
(to) cater for (to) provide services for
surge large sudden increase in something
readily easily and quickly

2 SKIM

a What is an advance factory unit?
b How can a company expand very quickly in Milton Keynes?

Now read the text and answer the skim questions.

B Look at these sections after reading the text:

3 COMPREHENSION

a What are the advantages of an advance factory unit?
b When is it possible for a company to surrender its factory lease?
c What have Hoechst built in Milton Keynes?
d What sort of company would prefer to lease a site and develop it itself?

4 INFERENCE

a Why does the text give a list of the names of companies who have moved to Milton Keynes? What effect should it have?
b What sort of special requirements might make a company want to lease a site instead of taking a ready-built factory?

5 REFERENCE

a What is the Development Corporation?
b Where is Milton Keynes? Where does the name come from?

6 LANGUAGE

Look at this sentence from the text:
  Milton Keynes offers **a wide range of** sites and premises for industrialists.
This combination of words is a collocation—a fixed phrase. If we used 'a big range', 'a large range' or 'a broad range' it would have the same meaning, but it would sound strange: everyone says a wide range of.
There are several collocations in the text. Try and find those which have these meanings:
a keep your cash invested
b bigger and bigger
c sensible and useful business idea
d great importance
e size of the business

7 OPINION

a Why does the Development Corporation offer to take back factory leases if a company wants to move? Isn't this a very expensive policy? How could it benefit the city?
b Do you think the city presents itself as an interesting business location? Would you be interested in moving your business there? Why?/Why not?
c What reasons do companies usually have for relocating their factories? What are the most important arguments in favour of relocation?

8 WRITING

a Write a letter to one of the companies mentioned in the text, explaining that you are thinking of moving to Milton Keynes, and that you would like to know how they feel about the city. You want to know whether they are glad they moved, whether there were any problems, and so on.
b Write a memo to your Finance Director, sending him the Milton Keynes brochure, and giving him a 200-word summary of the main points made in the text.

ANSWER KEY

UNIT 1
INFERENCE
a because the US government controls the number and type of products entering the country.
b the letters and numbers that will be on the boxes and packaging of the freight.
c The 425 refers to the wattage (and therefore the power) of the drill.

REFERENCE
a CIF = costs, insurance, freight
per pro = on behalf of
rpm = revolutions per minute
b Ltd is used in the UK—a Limited Company.
Inc is American—Incorporated.
c 12 and a half millimetres. In English, a full stop is used to show decimals, a comma is used to indicate thousands.

UNIT 2
INFERENCE
a probably to everybody who received the first free copy of the magazine, but did not return the application card.
b It is paid for by advertising. It is sent free to all the people who might want to buy the products advertised in the magazine.
c They want to encourage the reader to think it's a good magazine.

REFERENCE
a Enclosure—something is sent with the letter.
b *Public Works Review* seems to be a magazine that was taken over and is now part of *Civil Engineering*.

UNIT 3
INFERENCE
a to show that important, well-known companies think the Barbican is a good place for a conference.
b that the Barbican and BP work well together; that the Barbican is a perfect place for BP—and similarly for anyone else.
c because they will make the conference members happy, keep them interested, and help to make the conference a better experience.

REFERENCE
a BP = British Petroleum
b EC2 = East Central 2, a postal district of London
c City = the City of London, the business centre of London, which is very small. Most of central London is actually in the City of Westminster.

UNIT 4
INFERENCE
a because letters take a long time to get to the USA, and the customer might find another business partner in the meantime.

b You don't have to wait two weeks for a reply to the suggestions in your letter.
c It's more personal, and much quicker. It's also possible to make suggestions, or give prices, that you wouldn't want to write in a letter. On the phone a suggestion is less permanent, and you can change it quickly if the other person doesn't agree.

REFERENCE
a a type of cheese from France
b a type of cheese from Greece
c They are the names of time zones across the USA. Eastern includes New York and Washington, and is one hour ahead of Central, which includes Chicago. Mountain is one hour behind Central, and Pacific (which includes the West Coast) is one hour behind Mountain.
d the telephone system, often called Ma Bell. It has now been broken into smaller companies.

UNIT 5
INFERENCE
a It means it costs $5 to reach one thousand readers.
b Statistics show that *Time B* reaches a lot of people, and that these people are 100% business people, and with high incomes. This makes it more interesting for the advertisers who want to reach these people.
c *Business Week* is sold outside the USA, *Time B* only inside the USA. *Time B* also has non-business news, to make it a more interesting magazine.
d because college graduates usually have higher positions and more money to spend on the products advertised—or the power to make their company buy these products.

REFERENCE
a black and white
b the cost of placing an advertisement on one whole page.

UNIT 6
INFERENCE
a because they will solve most production problems— you don't have to think any more about it.
b FMC want you to think about the nature of problems, and how to solve them. This sort of problem could catch your attention, and make you think that FMC could solve your business problems.

REFERENCE
a California
b The (800) telephone numbers in the USA are free numbers, used by many companies in advertising. Whichever part of the country you are in, you can call this number *free* to get more information about the company. Since the offices are in California, there is also a California number.

UNIT 7

INFERENCE

a Sending free copies is a popular method of advertising and letting people see the magazine. It suggests that the magazine is not available in the shops, so people wouldn't normally see it. It could suggest the magazine is not selling well enough.

b This is a form letter, which is sent to everybody who shows an interest. Perhaps they forgot to up-date it this month.

c another encouragement, to make it easier to buy the magazine.

REFERENCE

a an invoice you pay before you get the goods. It protects the seller from non-payment.

b photocopier

UNIT 8

INFERENCE

a because many people will judge the quality of the product *inside* the container by the quality of the container itself.

b It's not clear, but these market surveys are probably carried out by Libbey's advertising agency, and thus paid for by Libbey's.

c in order to make Americans feel it would be more patriotic to buy these containers, rather than plastic made from imported oil.

REFERENCE

a a natural mineral, sodium carbonate: Na_2CO_3

b a journalist who also makes TV advertising commercials to sell Libbey products.

c A cocktail is a drink made from a mixture of different things. It used to be made only by a good barman, but now it is possible to buy the cocktails already mixed in a bottle.

UNIT 9

INFERENCE

a There are two classes for sending letters. First-class costs more, but delivery is quicker.

b because it saves labour costs at the post office, and looks like a discount to the customer.

c They show that important companies use this service.

REFERENCE

a V.P. = vice-president

b A ZIP code is a number, like 10029, which shows what town, and what part of the town, an address is in.

c Asst. = assistant; Svcs. = services; D.C. = District of Columbia

UNIT 10

INFERENCE

a that the work done in between the two pictures only takes five minutes with the new machine.

b correspondence—writing letters is the only work they all have in common.

c They are encouraged to think of the famous name, all the other products made, the company's reputation for reliability etc.

UNIT 11

INFERENCE

a British Association for Commercial and Industrial Education.

b It's a magazine about training, and it's *not* quarterly, so it's probably monthly.

c It suggests help and information, which can be obtained quickly and easily.

REFERENCE

a The B stands for British; the phone looks British.

b Surrey is a county south of London.

UNIT 12

INFERENCE

a You have to call the operator, and give your credit card number. Then they send the bill for the telephone call to your home.

b It's permanent. You automatically get a new one each year—if you pay your bills.

c No. You can only call *from* the USA or *to* the USA. You have to be connected to the American phone system.

REFERENCE

a C&P is the telephone company that used to own Bell. It has now become several smaller companies. It stands for Chesapeake and Potomac, referring to the bay and river around Washington D.C.

b a group of numbers at the end of an address, to show what part of the State or city you live in.

c the number of your town or city in the telephone system. The Area Code for New York is 212.

UNIT 13

INFERENCE

a It could be short of customers; or they have printed too many copies of Volume 1, and so they are using the extra copies for publicity.

b Normally scientific journals have a waiting period of 2–3 years before an article is published.

c because the other prices can change with the exchange rates.

REFERENCE

a Dfl. means Dutch florins, but the spoken name is Guilders.

UNIT 14

INFERENCE

a because they didn't want to lose control over decisions in the company. Keeping all the equity means you have more control.

b The service charge and the interest charge are not explained here. They could be high: it's not clear.

c an improvement in his cash flow.

REFERENCE

a a town in Scotland

b to check the accounts and be responsible to the board.

UNIT 15

INFERENCE

a The price might change, and then the circular would need re-printing. So it's only given on the order form.

b Travel agents don't get so much commission from a cheaper fare.

c It is suggesting that food in Moscow is usually bad.

REFERENCE

a normal fare, not charter or discount seats.

b Fleet Street is the home of British newspapers.

c Singapore dollars

UNIT 16

INFERENCE

a All the possibilities suggest cars are not so good.

b Business lunches often include a lot of alcohol.

c out of anger at the boss, the company, the weather, the long day.

REFERENCE

a Devon is a county in the south-west of Britain.

b Inter-City is the British Rail fast train service. The 125 is a train that goes at 125 miles per hour. A sleeper is a train you can get a couchette or bed on.

c a group of company cars that can be used by different members of staff.

d Plymouth is a town in the south-west of England.

UNIT 17

INFERENCE

a It is financed privately, but the director spent many years working for the government, so he may not be independent.

b The advisory committee will decide what is to be studied—so the members of the committee will make sure the studies do not conflict with their interests.

c Medium-term studies are important because an economic policy or action which operates in the medium-term (1 to 3 years) will have results within the life of one Presidential term. So a medium-term policy may help the President to get re-elected.

REFERENCE

a District of Columbia

b a large charitable foundation

c a government agency which gathers international intelligence in the interests of the country's defence.

UNIT 18

INFERENCE

a The city needs new jobs; each new business brings new jobs and extra tax income, which can be used to help more new businesses.

b mostly tax savings, cheap loans, cheap office space and so on.

c The city has the finance ready, and wants to encourage fast-moving new business.

REFERENCE

a There will be restrictions about the sort of or size of the business: if the business 'qualifies', it meets those conditions.

b a tax of 5% or 10%, for example, on the sale price of a product.

UNIT 19

INFERENCE

a They bring all the information together into a concise summary.

b Useful information is often in many different places—magazines, government reports and so on. The implication is that it is easier for a specialist service to 'watch' all these places for useful information, than it is for the individual.

REFERENCE

a Not only the name but also the address is the same.

b The work of the EEC—the European Economic Community.

UNIT 20

INFERENCE

a Perhaps advertising companies want to stop bad advertising, because if they didn't do it themselves, the government might want to control advertising.

b Bad advertising might make the public less influenced by good advertising, and so the business would suffer.

REFERENCE

a A priest of the Methodist church, a type of Protestant.

b A lord, baron, count, countess and so on, who by birth or by title given by the British government has the right to sit in the House of Lords and check the laws made by the House of Commons.

c Independent Broadcasting Authority

UNIT 21

INFERENCE

a He was very good at making deals, and he expanded at the right time.

b The store was bigger than was usual at that time.

c probably because it was a cheap purchase, which provided a large profit compared to the investment.

d He seems a little shy and modest, and more interested in working than in being rich.

REFERENCE

a 'O' levels are Ordinary level school exams taken in Britain at age 16.

b Discount warehouses sell well-known products at a low price, by reducing the service and store costs.

c selling shares to the public. This can bring a lot of capital into the company.

d international tennis competition for young players.

UNIT 22

INFERENCE

a The aim is to introduce the idea of quality circles to companies.

b It is assumed that people have heard what it is, and so it is not explained in the programme.

c He seems to be both: there is a reference to an examination paper he wrote for students.

d because the success of Japanese companies often seems to be greater, and British management would like to copy it.

REFERENCE

a perhaps some kind of consultancy.

b They produce pots, cups, and so on in a distinctive blue and white design.

c the national steel producing company in Britain.

d a college for 16–20 year old students doing practical training, and students doing diploma courses. It appears that David Hutchins works, or worked, there.

UNIT 23

INFERENCE

a one week

b probably a group of optional study subjects, from which you must choose one or two: you can choose them as freely as goods in a supermarket.

c to increase motivation during the course: you only do well if you know why you're doing it.

REFERENCE

a B.Sc. = Bachelor of Science
R & D = research and development
MBS = Manchester Business School
IEEE = Institute of Electrical and Electronic Engineers

b publishers

UNIT 24

INFERENCE

a good—earnings have increased.

b because it is people who design and make the products, and who make a good or bad impression on the customers.

c how much money they get, and how they feel they are treated.

d new regulations or taxes, legal restrictions on the nature of products, and so on.

UNIT 25

INFERENCE

a They probably said that Chadwick had to pay *its* bills—or at least that Chadwick could have less time to pay. The high cost of credit may have been the real cause of the change in their policy.

b If they have a lot of customers who do not pay quickly, they may have cash flow problems that would prevent them buying enough stock to meet everybody's orders.

REFERENCE

a the high cost of credit, and the difficulty in getting large amounts of credit.

b a letter sent automatically after a certain time, telling the customer that he/she should have paid the bill by now.

UNIT 26

INFERENCE

a They can prevent your business from being successful, if they don't try to find customers for you.

b the transfer of profits out of the country.

c They might try to sell your product in the wrong way, to the wrong people. In this way sales may be lower, since the people who need your product don't know about it.

REFERENCE

a A British company needs permission to invest its money outside Britain.

b for example, Sears, Bloomingdales

UNIT 27

INFERENCE

a so that anyone who wants to check the legal position can read exactly what was said, without any interpretation or adaptation.

b You would need to look for a particular subject in many different books.

c useful words, key words, that people might want to look for. They are there as a reference point.

REFERENCE

a a newspaper for the shipping business.

b f.o.b. = free on board

c EC4 means East Central section 4 of London. The other letters and numbers tell the postman which street the address is in. It's the post code (Zip in the USA).

UNIT 28

INFERENCE

a because it is spent discussing business and negotiating contracts.

b because people want to get to the office, and don't want to spend a long time eating.

c Most people are still a little tired or bad-tempered at breakfast time, and don't feel like having long conversations.

REFERENCE

a a brand of high quality drinking water, sold in bottles. It comes from France, and is very expensive.

b people like singers, actors and musicians who work late at night in clubs and theatres. Also the people who go to the theatres and clubs on Broadway to watch them.

c Downtown is the financial centre of New York, in the southern part of Manhattan, and uptown is the expensive, smart areas like Park Avenue, further north. Midtown is the part in the middle.

UNIT 29

INFERENCE

a Some civil servants have power and influence, because they are in charge of spending government money. If there is no public spending, they would have no power or influence. They want the government to spend.

b Perhaps the writer is referring to the British governmental system, which usually involves the two major parties alternating the role of government.

REFERENCE

a OPEC = Organisation of Petroleum Exporting Countries
OECD = Organisation for Economic Cooperation and Development

b gross domestic product

c perhaps British Information Service; or Business Information Service. The S could also be Statistics.

UNIT 30

INFERENCE

a because it hasn't prosecuted many companies for breaking the law, probably because the law is not clear.

b Manufacturers make more money by selling to small independent retailers, who do not buy in bulk, and so do not get a big discount. The manufacturers also want to protect the small shops, since they are found in more towns than the discounters. This gives the manufacturer a wider distribution of sales and market coverage.

c There could be many practices that are 'anti-competitive'—the term is not specific enough.

d They could pretend they were out of stock, or send faulty goods.

REFERENCE

a Argos sells via a catalogue. Tesco is a supermarket company, selling mainly cheap food.

b Hotpoint is an equipment manufacturer. Comet is a discount warehouse.

UNIT 31

INFERENCE

a because companies didn't think the idea was very interesting until they saw the results of using quality circles in Japan, and were impressed by its success.

b probably because they made an agreement with the unions which neither of them want to show in public, as it might make future discussions more difficult.

c perhaps the workers felt they were not consulted, that their ideas were not welcome. Probably there was bad worker-management communication.

REFERENCE

a Queen's Counsel, a type of barrister (lawyer)

b the state of New York (not the city, which is NYC)

c the union of workers in car factories

d an aeroplane manufacturer. It is obvious from the reference to F-5 fighter planes.

UNIT 32

INFERENCE

a the death of selling in British businesses.

b He thinks they have not tried hard enough to sell their products.

c You must identify the right market before you can sell effectively; but when you do find the market, you must sell hard.

d The managers probably didn't plan correctly, or didn't inform or motivate their sales force properly.

REFERENCE

a It studies what is happening in science and technology, and how this affects business. It makes suggestions as to how science and technology could be used more effectively.

b A senior teacher at a university (the title is not used everywhere).

UNIT 33

INFERENCE

a to avoid the company having to pay income tax.

b if the profits are less than £1,500 in one year.

REFERENCE

a in the English Channel. They are semi-independent, but part of Britain.

b a shareholder representing someone else and appointed by that person.

c Individuals pay income tax; companies pay corporation tax.

d another island in the English Channel, smaller than Jersey.

e a tax on the making of official documents.

UNIT 34

INFERENCE

a because it was better than the competing products. It was also cheaper, because Hewlett-Packard was still a small company with low overheads.

b It developed the idea of time-sharing in computers.

c electronic data products—computers and similar things.

REFERENCE

a It is in California, where it became famous for producing very good electronics engineers, who set up new industries in Silicon Valley, the area where new computer and microchip companies have built factories.

b cartoon films—Mickey Mouse, Donald Duck and so on.

UNIT 35

INFERENCE

a It should make the reader feel that Milton Keynes must be a good place to go to.

b If a company needs a very big factory, or a factory which has to have special equipment in it (which could mean special types of floor or walls), it might want to lease a site.

REFERENCE

a the part of the local government which gives financial help to new companies coming to the town. It is responsible for bringing new companies and jobs into the town.

b north of London. The name comes partly from the famous economist, Keynes.

GLOSSARY

The numbers refer to the unit where the word is explained.

touch wood	16	understatement	14	versatility	10	weed out	20
trappings	21	undertake	23	vintage	8	weedy	30
trial offer	7	unremitting	28	vital	22	well-placed	33
trim	29	updating	7	vitality	18	wheels of Brie	4
turned up trumps	21	vary	15	vocational	11	wining	16
turnover	14	verbatim	27	warehouse	1	yours faithfully	7